T0104309

DEARLY BELOVED

HOW GOD'S LOVE FOR HIS CHURCH
DEEPENS OUR LOVE FOR EACH OTHER

VERMON PIERRE

MOODY PUBLISHERS
CHICAGO

Scripture quotations are from the ESV® Bible (The Holy Bible, English Standard Version®), © 2001 by Crossway, a publishing ministry of Good News Publishers. Used by permission. All rights reserved. The ESV text may not be quoted in any publication made available to the public by a Creative Commons license. The ESV may not be translated in whole or in part into any other language.

All emphasis in Scripture has been added.

Edited by Pamela J. Pugh
Interior design: Ragont Design
Cover design: Erik M. Peterson
Cover graphic of color wave copyright © 2023 by Alicia Bock/Stocksy (4078665). All rights reserved.
Author photo: Tara Nichole Photo

Library of Congress Cataloging-in-Publication Data

Names: Pierre, Vermon, author.
Title: Dearly beloved : how God's love for his church deepens our love for each other / Vermon Pierre.
Description: Chicago : Moody Publishers, [2024] | Includes bibliographical references. | Summary: "We are caught in a love story. The Bible describes our relationship with God as a marriage. But what exactly does that mean? Pierre ushers us into an understanding of that beautiful, life-giving relationship. Learn how you are loved, how to love God, and how to love one another"-- Provided by publisher.
Identifiers: LCCN 2023029548 (print) | LCCN 2023029549 (ebook) | ISBN 9780802428592 (paperback) | ISBN 9780802475190 (ebook)
Subjects: LCSH: Love--Religious aspects--Christianity. | Interpersonal relations--Religious aspects--Christianity. | God (Christianity)--Love.
Classification: LCC BV4639 .P525 2024 (print) | LCC BV4639 (ebook) | DDC 241/.4--dc23/eng/20230908
LC record available at https://lccn.loc.gov/2023029548
LC ebook record available at https://lccn.loc.gov/2023029549

Originally delivered by fleets of horse-drawn wagons, the affordable paperbacks from D. L. Moody's publishing house resourced the church and served everyday people. Now, after more than 125 years of publishing and ministry, Moody Publishers' mission remains the same—even if our delivery systems have changed a bit. For more information on other books (and resources) created from a biblical perspective, go to www.moodypublishers.com or write to:

Moody Publishers
820 N. LaSalle Boulevard
Chicago, IL 60610

1 3 5 7 9 10 8 6 4 2

Printed in the United States of America

To my beloved wife, Dennae

To my beloved church, Roosevelt Community Church

CONTENTS

Introduction

TO BETTER IMAGINE, FEEL, AND LIVE OUT GOD'S LOVE

I think one of the easiest ways to convince a child that there is such a thing as magic is to introduce them to a magnet.

It's been a while for sure, but I still recall my sense of wonder and awe the first time I held a magnet in my hands. To feel the sudden "pull" when I brought the metallic material toward the magnet. A teacher later explained how it worked. If you place the right material in front of a magnet, the two will automatically stick together and stay that way. This doesn't happen with all materials, though. A magnet won't stick to fabric or wood. And in some cases there seems to be an invisible force that repels the magnet away from another material. For example, if you bring a strong magnet by water you will see the water move away from it.

Any leader who has tried to create and maintain unity within a local church knows both the highs and lows of such efforts. At times it seems everyone is on the same page, easily and happily united. Everyone "sticks" together. But at other times it seems almost impossible to keep people united. No matter what you try, they just won't "stick" together. And even worse, there are times when the magnetic momentum of the community has turned into people pushing away from one another rather than drawing to one another.

The sad reality is there are more repelling tendencies rather than attracting tendencies in our current cultural moment. Ezra Klein writes in *Why We're Polarized* about how we have split into competing identity groups that have only strengthened in their polarization.[1] People increasingly find their own sense of self from how they are unlike others and from their public opposition to those groups that are not part of their particular identity group.

A DIFFERENT WAY

This polarization is not just within the broader culture; it is also within the church. Certainly, the church has long faced the problem of keeping competing identity groups united.[2] These problems remain with us today, but are now more visible and powerfully reinforced through the internet and social media. We split along multiple lines and have used technology to entrench within our bases. The magnetic force has swung firmly in the direction of repulsion and has only gotten stronger.

But it doesn't have to stay like this. The church can show a different way. This happens if we as the church can generate a force among us strong enough to attract people to one another, to unite people to one another in spite of polarizing tendencies. A force strong enough even to overcome the repelling force of our competing identity groups and create a community that would be a uniquely prophetic witness and presence within today's world.

The answer we are looking for to form a community like this begins with God. The church only exists because of Him. And it's in "how" God brought about the church that's the key to solving the problem of disunity and division. God united Himself to us in Christ, and He did this out of love. It's because God so loved the world that He gave His Son on our behalf, to save us and reconcile us to God (John 3:16; Eph. 2:4–5; 1 John 4:9–10).

> **If we are united to God in love, so also we are united to one another in love. Unity is not something we need to look for; unity is something we already have.**

God's love for us initiated and brought about our salvation and subsequent union to Him. As a result, unity is not something we need to look for; unity is something we already have. By faith in Christ we are already united to God.

And so if we are united to God most especially in love, so also we are united to one another in love. God's love for us in Christ is the only force strong enough to bring us together to God. And God's love in Christ is the only force strong enough to keep us together with God as one community in Christ.

Love is, of course, at the heart of everything for Christians. The only thing that "counts" for the Christian is "faith working through love" (Gal. 5:6). Love is the home for all of God's commandments (Gal. 5:14). If we are to be united it will only be because we are "united to one another in love" (Westminster Confession 26.1).

There is, however, a particular way to talk about the love of God that is especially helpful for thinking about unity with God and with one another. And it is the way in which God loves us as a husband loves his bride.

Our relationship with God, and specifically the Lord Jesus, is regularly referred to in the Bible as being a marriage (e.g., Isa. 54:5–6; 62:4–5; Hos. 2:19–20; John 3:28–29). And as we read in Revelation 19:7 and other passages, it's the one and only marriage that will last forever.

> This is the kind of love that exists between God and the church: affectionate and committed. And love is the key to unity.

And in that marriage we are loved by the Lord with a marital kind of love. When Paul tells husbands in Ephesians 5:25 that they are to love their wives, he tells them to do so in the same way that "Christ loved the church." Paul goes on to explain that the profound mystery of human marriage is that it is a reflection of the marriage between Christ and the church (Eph. 5:32). And so love within human marriage is a reflection of the love between the Lord God and His bride, the church.

The Bible uses this metaphor because the marriage relationship uniquely evokes the most powerful expressions of love—specifically an affectionate, committed love. This is the kind of love that exists between God and the church. It's out of this kind of love that we must love one another within the church. Love is the key to unity. Love is what united us to God. And love, namely God's love, is what we need to unite us to one another.

BEYOND THE SUPERFICIAL

When it comes, then, to figuring out how best to love one another, it will begin with God. We love based on the love the Lord shows toward us (1 John 4:7, 12), which means we love out of and within God's love for us. And since God's love for us as His bride is such a unifying power, then this is the kind of way we want to love one another as a unifying power among us. We want to love one another in the same way God, as a husband, loves us, as His bride.

Marital love is not the most immediate metaphor you might think of if someone were to ask you what it means to love one another. If you asked a Christian for an illustration on loving other Christians, they might talk about loving someone with the same passion you have for a sports team, or with the same sacrificial commitment that you have for your children. But loving others like you do in a marriage includes all the things we have just mentioned and includes even more than that. Marital love gives us the most embodied, practically realized, fully encompassing expression of love for our church relationships. It gives us the most committed, in-depth version of love. It is the kind of love that has the broadest and most effective tools for nurturing and strengthening our relationships with one another.

Now, obviously, a "marital" kind of love within the church isn't going to be expressed in exactly or all the same ways love is expressed within an actual human marriage. The physical expressions of love, for example, rightfully (and thankfully!) stay within the bounds of a one husband–one wife marriage.

That said, we do well to embrace the meaning and sensibility behind marital love when we consider what it means to love one another within the church. Divine love, in all its expansive, affective, and intimate power, is the power we must fully understand and tap into for how we love God and one another. Love like this will bring true fellowship and deeper and more robust unity within the church. It can bring a holistic devotion to Jesus and one another. Christians who love one another like this will better resist the natural drift toward superficial faith and shallow fellowship and the forces of today's current polarization and division.

We are in a time where people are already divided and becoming even more divided from one another with each passing news event and social media post. If local church communities want to be united in the midst of this division, they must learn to love one another. And they must do so in a way that is not abstract or superficial or cliché. We must love each other in the strongest way the Bible talks about love—through the imagery and language of marriage. This is how we can have a community of people who don't simply put up with each other or who remain superficial with each other but rather love each other with the kind of passion and commitment that is echoed in the best marriages.

WHAT IS POSSIBLE

Love like this is hard. Especially when the community is made up of men and women, of young and old, of people from different races and ethnicities and social classes. The history of our country and the current cultural climate suggest that being authentically beloved to one another is close to impossible. Bring different people together, and it seems the eventual inevitable result is repulsion rather than attraction to each other.

The church I lead has long been known as one of the more diverse churches in the Phoenix metro area. It's something I've been proud of and frankly took for granted. I never thought our diversity could "hurt" us. And yet during the past several years, I have seen just how tenuous unity within diversity can be. Differences over politics and race caused even long-term friendships to falter or worse, fall apart. It's led to many people deciding to leave the church, to find spaces where people were more culturally and politically or even racially like them, rather than embracing a diverse-in-Christ community. In some ways, this was not surprising. Our country has spent most of its history having racially segregated churches. Polarization and division is our default mode. What we see happening is just the latest expression of age-old patterns of behavior.

If we want to break this pattern, we will need to reclaim the Bible's vision of community: one where people from all kinds of backgrounds can be in one church and relate to each other and stay in relationship with each other, even through differences, even with periodic times of tension, even after misunderstandings and mistakes.

This is possible for the church. We can form communities of diverse people who overcome our historic and current tendencies to form separate, polarized identity groups. We can form communities of diverse people who instead come together and stay together—in close, dare we say intimate, ways. That is, as long as we can love one another. As long as we can be beloved to one another. And that will happen as we draw from the reality that we already are beloved to Jesus. Let's remember, the Bible tells a love story of God pursuing His people, even in their rejection and infidelity toward Him, even in their separation from God and one another, eventually saving His people and culminating in Jesus marrying His bride, the church, and living with her forever. Because of that love story with Christ, we can believe and live our love story with one another.

In the following chapters, we will look at community and what it means to love one another through the lens of God's marital love for us. In the first chapter we will survey and reflect on the biblical metaphor of God being married to His people. In the second chapter we will show how our being loved by God as our husband connects to how we then love one another. In the succeeding chapters we will apply what we've seen in chapters 1 and 2. Some of the ways we will do this will be familiar areas. For example, we will talk about taking initiative. We'll discuss the power of words in our relationships. We will talk about this, however, through the lens of us being the beloved spouse of the Lord. Other areas will be new ways to think about loving one another. For example, we will look at how intimacy and delight factor into our interpersonal relationships within the church.

Through all these reflections, the result I hope for is that we better imagine, feel, and live out God's love for us such that we are drawn that much closer together in His love.

Part 1

HOW WE ARE BELOVED

Chapter 1

BELOVED TO THE LORD

After a full day of activities with my friends and family, I was finally alone.

I was by myself for these last few hours before I would head to the church. I had been waiting for this moment since I knew that Dennae was the woman I wanted to marry. And now the moment was finally here. My life would dramatically change in only a few hours' time.

And it really did change. From the moment I said "I do," my life was bound up with a woman who would never again be only "a woman" to me but instead be "my wife." Everything I thought about myself, how I moved through the world, how I experienced my successes and failures, they would all now happen in the context of marriage to this specific woman.

Marriage is a uniquely defining relationship because of how thoroughly and profoundly it touches every aspect of who you are and how you live. We are living in a time when marriage is sometimes seen as insignificant. With increasing rates of cohabitation, marriage can be treated as just a more formal way to finalize living with someone. Yet even with those trends, marriage still stands out because of how it uniquely lays a claim on a person's life. It's what makes marriage unlike any other relationship.

Entering into marriage is not just deciding to be lifelong roommates with someone. It is not simply agreeing to share some common hobbies with someone. It is something much more mystical and magical. Marriage is becoming one with another person. Your whole self unites with the whole self of someone else, creating a new community, or unit, of persons. Marriage is a committed relationship of love and fellowship that will be particular to the people in that relationship. It is a relationship of commitment and love that shapes and defines you in the context of your relationship with your spouse.

It's striking then to consider that marriage is the metaphor used to describe the relationship we have with the Lord. That we, God's people, can be said to be *married* to God. The Lord God of the Bible, the one true God, is thoroughly and fully united to us and we to Him. God willingly enters into a new space when He forms a relationship with us, wherein who we are and who God is from that point on is shaped and defined by this new relationship.

VIVID, NOT VAGUE

Marriage isn't the only metaphor used in the Bible to describe the relationship of God to His people. God is rightly described as being a king over us. God can also be said to be our shepherd. He is also father to us. These are all important metaphors to help us understand how we relate to Him. However, out of all the ways to describe how God is toward us, arguably the most distinctive and striking metaphor is to say that God is a husband to us.

It's worth noting here that Judaism is the only faith in which the nation, rather than a goddess or some representative individual female, was the bride of their god. The way pagan people talked about or related to their gods was much different. Their gods were self-centered and manipulated humans for their own benefit. People could only hope to convince their gods to be good to them, and so they offered sacrifices in exchange for the favors they sought. The pagan relationship with gods was one of struggle, each party vying for control in order to get what they wanted.

> **The story that holds the universe together is the love story of God seeking after, finding, and then marrying His people.**

But with Yahweh, the God of the Bible, we have something unique. Here we see human beings having a relationship with God marked not by manipulation or coercion. This relationship is not superficial or primarily transactional. Instead, the Bible speaks of human beings having a relationship with God characterized by unity. By intimacy. By commitment. By love.

It says something about the very nature of reality that the One who created everything wants to be so close to us, so connected to us, that the best way to describe this strong desire on His part is that He wants to be married to us. The story that holds the universe together, the story that angels watch with excitement and eagerly retell to one another as they sit around the campfires of heaven, is the love story of God seeking after, finding, and then marrying His people. A story that culminates in His people being together with Him in a forever union of fellowship and love.

Jonathan Edwards writes, "The creation of the world seems to have been especially for this end, that the eternal Son of God might obtain a spouse, towards whom he might fully exercise the infinite benevolence of his nature, and to whom he might, as it were, open and pour forth all that immense foundation of condescension, love, and grace that was in his heart, and that in this way God might be glorified."[1]

It does feel a bit strange to talk this way about God. To say that we are "married" to God? It's strange to imagine, much less say out loud.

But maybe that's because of how abstract our understanding of God and His love tends to be. We tend to talk and think in vague ways about having a relationship of love with God. If I were to ask you what you immediately think about when you hear someone say, "God loves you," what comes to mind? Some kind of shimmery image of an actor who has played Jesus smiling at you? An old man in a white robe giving you a hug or a couple of good pats on the back to show how he's happy to be with you?

The thing is, the Bible doesn't give us vague or trite descriptions when it says that God loves us. The Bible talks in direct and vivid language on this topic. If we want to understand what God's love is, and understand it at its purest, strongest, most enduring and intimate level, we must talk about His love through the metaphor of marriage—that God loves His people as a husband should love his wife.

THE STORY BEGINS

We can start by looking in the Old Testament. Here we see God clearly described as being husband of His people, which was the nation of Israel at that time.

God intentionally establishes a relationship with Israel, beginning with their ancestor Abraham and his family. Later, God rescues Israel from captivity in Egypt and then establishes a covenant with the people at Sinai, ratifying it through sacrifice. The people then set off into the wilderness, with God leading them, providing food and water for them all along the way until He brings them to a home in Canaan, a fertile and rich land. These are the basic elements of the story of the beginning of the relationship between God and Israel. And notably, all the elements in this story are the elements that make up the beginnings of a marriage.

The story begins with God initiating toward Israel, making an official commitment on Mount Sinai by establishing a covenant with them. This covenant is akin to a formal marriage commitment. God and Israel were to be exclusive to each other, living with each other, committed only to each other. They had certain obligations in the relationship: God leading, protecting, and providing for His people, and His people honoring and submitting to God's loving leading and care.

Old Testament professor Seock-Tae Sohn has noted that many scholars talk about how the Sinai covenant is set up like an ancient Hittite political treaty. This isn't a wrong comparison. However, it is not the only background to this covenant. The covenant established between God and Israel is also found in ancient marriage customs, which were a form of covenant. (For example, see Malachi 2:14.) Indeed, the covenant that God establishes between Himself and Israel is explicitly referred to as a marriage.[2] Consider these passages:

> "When I passed by you again and saw you, behold, you were at the age for love, and I spread the corner of my garment over you and covered your nakedness; I made my vow to you and entered into a covenant with you, declares the Lord GOD, and you became mine." (Ezek. 16:8)

"And I will betroth you to me forever. I will betroth you
to me in righteousness and in justice, in steadfast love
and in mercy. I will betroth you to me in faithfulness.
And you shall know the LORD." (Hos. 2:19–20)

We find many other references to God being married to His
people. The Sinai covenant is, in effect, a wedding ceremony between Yahweh and Israel. The covenant meal that the seventy
elders of Israel had in front of Yahweh after making covenant on
Mount Sinai is the wedding feast confirming and celebrating the
union.[3] Jeremiah 2 portrays the jour-
ney of Yahweh leading Israel through
the wilderness to Canaan after the
exodus as being like a bridegroom
who brings his bride to his home from
her father's house after the engagement.[4] In other places in Jeremiah,
God refers to Israel as His beloved
(Jer. 11:15; 12:7).

> **God makes it clear
> that the Israelites will
> belong to Him and be
> His people. However,
> they will belong to
> Him in a special way.**

This covenantal phrase is often
found in the Old Testament: "I will be
your God and you shall be my people" (Lev. 26:12). This phrase
is like the phrase said in Jewish wedding contracts: "She is my
wife and I am her husband from this day and forever."[5]

God's covenant with Israel was a commitment to Israel. God
makes it clear that the Israelites will belong to Him and be His
people (Ex. 6:7a; Lev. 26:12). However, they will belong to Him
in a special way. God will not treat His people as His property
or playthings or slaves—these are all ways that other "gods" are
described as treating their people. Rather, the Israelites are cher-
ished and desired by God. They are more than objects or playthings or slaves; they are as a beloved wife to Him.

I've had the privilege of officiating at many weddings. One of my favorite parts of the ceremony is getting a front row seat when the groom first sees his bride walking down the aisle. The groom's attention is fixed on his bride. He looks on her with delight and affection, with eager anticipation for her to make her way to him so that finally they can be married and be together from that day on. That's how the Lord looks upon His people—with delight and excitement. They are His "treasured possession" (Deut. 14:2), His beloved bride that He freely and fully loves.

A NEW COVENANT—A NEW MARRIAGE

There is, though, an unfortunate dark side to this marriage story: the continuing failure of Israel to be faithful to God. God was the initiating committed husband who took Israel "by the hand to bring them out of Egypt"; nevertheless, Israel soon afterward would break her covenant with Him (Jer. 31:31–32).

Throughout her history, Israel breaks her covenant by worshiping idols and the gods of the surrounding pagan nations, actions the Bible starkly describes as tantamount to committing adultery. Again, the metaphor used here is striking. Out of all the ways to describe how Israel has been uncommitted to God, the Bible uses the most severe image possible to describe Israel's sin against Him. The image of adultery doesn't allow us to think that Israel just let God down, as if Israel simply failed to do the dishes a few times. Rather, it speaks of violated intimacy and personal betrayal. It's a metaphor that reinforces just how close God considers Himself to His people. So close, that only serial adultery can describe what it is like when Israel follows other gods besides the Lord God.

Given Israel's actions, God had every right to abandon Israel, to permanently divorce her, because of her unfaithfulness to him.[6]

But that's not what happens. God instead recommits to Israel. He calls Israel back to Himself, even after sending her away (Jer. 3:12, 14). His desire to be in close relationship with her is so strong and enduring, He promises to find a way whereby His people can be in relationship with Him, a relationship no longer threatened by idolatrous infidelity and betrayal but instead one that endures and flourishes in righteousness and faithfulness and love (Hos. 2:19–20).

> **That God comes to us in Jesus emphasizes like nothing else the strength and fervor of God's love for us. It says that we are dearly loved by Him, that we are beloved to Him.**

We see God follow through on this promise as we move from the Old Testament into the New Testament. The relationship between God and His people opens up from being between God and Israel to being between God, more specifically Jesus, and the church. The coming of Jesus is the fulfillment of the promise given in Jeremiah 31:31–34. A new covenant—a new marriage—is formed, carried out, and fulfilled in Jesus as the promised Messiah who willingly gives Himself up in order to save and redeem His bride, the church (Eph. 5:25).

That God comes to us in Jesus emphasizes like nothing else the strength and fervor of God's love for us. It says that we are dearly loved by Him, that we are beloved to Him.

God in Jesus loves us so much, He assumes humanity into Himself to make it possible for us to have a relationship with Him. God in Jesus passes through the crucible of suffering, pain, and death so that we can finally have a committed relationship with Him that will actually last and endure. The following verses flesh out the metaphor.

In John 3:27–30, John the Baptist sees himself as the friend who sets things up for Jesus, who is explicitly said to be the bridegroom coming for His bride.

Paul gives instructions on marriage in Ephesians 5:22–23, and in doing so makes clear that human marriage is ultimately a reflection of a divine reality, namely the marriage between Christ and His church. The actions of Jesus are in essence the actions of a husband who, out of love for his spouse, gives up all of himself for her sake.

Second Corinthians 11:2 tells us that the church should be like a pure virgin wife to Jesus. Jesus relates to the church and loves the church like a husband does his new wife.

And at the end of the Bible, in Revelation 19:6–9 and 21:9–11, we see that this divine relationship persists to eternity. All earthly marriages eventually end. But one marriage will endure forever, because it is a heavenly marriage. It is the marriage between the Lord and the church.

No other book of the Bible captures the full extent of God's love for us like the Song of Songs. I used to snicker to myself when reading this book as a kid. I couldn't believe I was actually reading such explicit language like this, let alone in a Bible that my parents had given me!

Once I became a proper seminarian, I became a more "sophisticated" exegete. I was taught to see the Song of Songs as singing the praises of human romance, as a celebration of the coming together of a man and woman in marriage.

But now, many years later, I'm seeing that there is more behind it than only human romance, for human marriages are designed to mirror heavenly marriage (Eph. 5:32). So the human marriage depicted in the Song of Songs, like all human marriages should be, is ultimately an echo and pointer to the heavenly marriage between the Lord Jesus and the church.

And what do we see about marriage in the Song of Songs? We

see commitment. Initiative. Affection and desire. Intimacy. We see love, the beloved love unique to marriage.

All of these things are reflections, echoes, signposts of what the church has in her relationship with the Lord. The Song of Songs' highly expressive description of marriage is a window into the "exclusive, eros love of God that overflows for his bride."[7]

> **To be known by God and to be loved by God is to be beloved to God.**

Let's again acknowledge how strange this feels, to talk about God and Jesus in this way. To say that we are in an intimate, affectionate "marital" relationship with God? This feels like we are on the precipice of falling into the clutches of a weird cult.

But there is something important to remember here. This is not a one-to-one metaphorical analogy. Human marriages operate in the physical world, while the heavenly marriage originates and comes out of the spiritual world. So, for example, there clearly is no one-to-one equivalent of physical sexual union. We aren't talking about people one day lining up in heaven one by one to physically kiss God. As Eric Ortlund puts it, "In fact, the Song was not meant to teach that there is something sexual about God; human sexuality is a good but entirely ordinary created thing."[8] The love of the Lord for us that we are talking about here is holy and pure and spiritual.

That being said, the intentional mention of human marriage being ultimately about heavenly marriage is not a throwaway metaphor. Human love in marriage, with all that it entails and implies, including its intimate and romantic dimensions, really is a key way to capture what it is to be loved by God, to be beloved to Him. It is a reflection of the divine.[9]

It says something very real about the relationship between

us and God. As such, when we consider human marriage and all that makes up human marriage, we are seeing something that spiritually and directly connects to how we relate to God.

To be known by God and to be loved by God is to be beloved to God. It is to know, sense, and feel His love for us as a dearly loved spouse. One who loves us even unto death itself, beyond even death itself.[10] One who loves us with the committed, fierce, strong, intimate intensity of a beloved spouse.

All of which means then that ultimate reality—the life we are heading into and will live in together—is best understood as living with God, being married to Jesus, loving God and being loved by God forever.

I've long enjoyed playing video games. And one game I have played a lot over the years is Madden NFL. I've enjoyed it as it has been my one way of ensuring that my New York Jets win the majority of their games. When I play Madden, my Jets always end up becoming a Super Bowl champion dynasty, winning at least four years in a row. It's a real and legit thrill to me. But even I, a superfan, have to admit that it's not reality (certainly not as of this writing). The video game is enjoyable, but what I really yearn for one day is the Jets, in real life, winning games and eventually winning the Super Bowl for the first time since 1969.

JESUS' LOVE: A BELOVED LOVE

This life we live now is significant and important. But even it is ultimately a temporary expression of an ensuing, enduring reality that is best described as us, united to God in Christ, living a married life with Him forever. Indeed, this life will one day be seen as a brief and passing rest stop compared to the final destination of abundant life and blessing (see 2 Cor. 4:17).

We begin married life with the Lord the moment we put our

faith in Jesus. And that moment we begin a life together with Him, that new life only grows and deepens and expands. The end of all things is not "cold dark blank space," as Ray Ortlund writes, but instead being with "a God above with love in his eyes for us and infinite joy to offer us."[11]

We can't now fully grasp all of what this will entail. Nevertheless, it is still quite significant to know that the best life the universe offers us feels like being married to someone who intimately, deeply, and fully loves us, and will love us like that forever.

This is the life into which all believers are headed. But we can already experience some of this life now. For already, in this life, the church is the bride of Christ even as we look to and prepare for when we will officially be His bride forever . . . which means that already right now we have poured into us from God abundant love, enduring commitment, and full intimacy. Already right now we swim in God's beloved love, flowing from God to us and eventually carrying all of us into eternity.

All of how we interact with one another, all of how we relate to one another, comes out of how God first related to us.

But now here is something to consider. This love, that flows from God to us, also flows among us. God's beloved love for you connects you to God in His beloved love *and* it connects you to other believers in the same beloved love. We are carried together with other believers into eternity in God's beloved love because God already today connects us together in His beloved love.

What makes us come together as the people of God and remain the people of God is what we have been given from God. We are family to one another because of God's adopting us into His family. We are brother and sister not because we naturally have divine DNA within us but because of what has been done for us, namely God putting us in the Son. We relate to one another not through any natural blood relations but through the spiritual blood relation that we gained through the shed blood of Jesus. It is the blood of Jesus that gives us the same spiritual DNA that makes us family.

We are a reconciled community to one another because God reconciled us to Himself. We can speak of unity among us, of being "one new man," because of what God has given us: the body and blood of Jesus (Eph. 2:13–16). This lasts into eternity even as it echoes back into the present, and in how we relate to one another today.

All of how we interact with one another, all of how we relate to one another, comes out of how God first related to us. We see, feel, and relate to one another in and through and out of God, and specifically in and through and out of Jesus.

This has implications for how we understand what it means to love one another within the church. We love one another from and out of God's love for us. And God loves us most distinctly and especially as a husband. He loves us with a beloved love, which means then that we love one another from and out of God's beloved love.

As we explore in the next chapter what it means to love one another, what we'll be talking about is loving one another with the love of God. Since the ultimate way God loves us is with a beloved love, then we need to consider the ways in which our love for each other is like this beloved love.

For Jesus' love at its heart is a beloved love.

Chapter 2

BELOVED TO ONE ANOTHER

Almost from birth, we begin to notice others.

In the early weeks of a baby's life she is noticing the faces around her, learning to respond and react to certain ones, like those of her parents. My wife and I had our fifth child in 2021. It was amazing to watch how quickly she recognized our faces and the faces of her siblings. I'd experienced this already with our other children, but it remains marvelous to see a new life first notice you and then react especially and uniquely to you as their parent.

It continues from there. Young children will soon notice differences in gender, skin color, language, speaking tones. At an early point, it morphs into more than noticing. Now they not only uniquely respond to you, they also will respond in different ways to other people.

As children grow and move into grade school, then middle school, and eventually high school and their teen years, their noticing will take on many of the social cues of our society. They will learn to make assessments based on what they notice. For example, they may notice someone talking differently than they're used to or enjoying music or investing in hobbies that are new or unfamiliar to them.

As time goes on, and especially as children's experiences expand and become more deeply embedded into existing social groups and structures and cultures, that assessment becomes a judgment.

It's not only that people talk differently from you, you now judge them because of those differences. It's not only that they listen to different music than you do, you now judge them based on their tastes in music, or on how they get their news, or on any number of things.

Such judgment becomes the basis of separation, of a preference to be with people who are similar to us. It's not that we dislike those who are different, it's just that we feel more comfortable with people who are more like we are. And in today's world, being comfortable is everything.

ON EQUAL GROUND

This is true in general, and it is true within the church. I have led a multiethnic church for nearly twenty years. It's one of the few multiethnic churches in our area led by a minority pastor. I used to think that the diversity of the church was a draw. Yet time has proven that while it is initially a draw—there is always something attractive about meeting someone new and different—over time it actually becomes a strain.

People in a diverse church gradually become aware of the differences they have with the other people in the room. Some differences are casual but others are quite profound. What was initially interesting and engaging becomes annoying and uncomfortable. And as more of those differences surface, and especially as tensions emerge out of those differences, the more inclined people will be to move toward what is familiar and similar. Why go through the awkwardness of talking to a mentally challenged homeless person when you can instead share parenting tips with the upwardly mobile middle-class couple who has children the same ages as yours?

We know it should be different in the church. I can quote Jesus' prayer, that we may be one (John 17:21) with the best of them. I have preached about how we are the "one new man" of Ephesians 2:15 more times than I can count. The church being "one" is a bedrock teaching and belief. Yet the church actually *being one* is much harder to attain and even harder to hold on to.

Unity in the church is supposed to go beyond the mere level of people showing up at the same place once a week and then leaving, not interacting with one another until next week. Unity is more than shared affinities or shared hobbies or a common stage of life.

Unity within the church is shown by a community of people made up of every tribe, language, and nation. It is a unity that crosses over every social barrier, every cultural dividing line, every race gap and gender gap and age gap, bringing people from across every social and cultural groupings possible into the one common community that we call the church. This is what the church fundamentally is: one cross-cultural, cross-social, cross-ethnic, cross-generational united community.

But for this to happen, we need to cultivate the kind of relationships within the church that are strong enough to unite us together across tribes, languages, and nations; relationships that are magnetic and attractive enough to overcome our personal preferences and biases; relationships that are stable enough to hold us together even when navigating through the inevitable conflicts and tensions that crop up when differing peoples are brought together in close relationship.

A unity like this needs people to adopt a posture toward one another that regularly inclines them toward one another. It needs people interacting with each other in ways that bond them to one another. It needs people who willingly, gladly, choose to be in relationship with one another.

Beloved love **is a love that orients us to see one another as Jesus does, namely as a beloved spouse.**

The one thing that does this, that gives us this posture and inclination, that provides this kind of solidifying and stabilizing relationship, is love. For there to be the most robust unity, the most cross-cultural unity, people must actively and generously love one another.

We must love each other in a way that overcomes our differences. We must love each other in contrast to our tendencies to judge and separate from one another. We must love in ways that incline us toward one another, indeed that unites us to one another. Love "is the great unifying force of life."[1]

It's not just any kind of love that will work here. A love that is only at the level of how you might feel about your favorite TV show or sports team or band or hobby or pillow won't work. Unity like this is only achieved if our love for one another is the strongest, most passionate expression of love.

The love we need that can unify people is what I called in the previous chapter a *beloved love*. It's a love that orients us to see one another as Jesus does, namely as a beloved spouse, and to relate to other believers as being beloved to you, because Jesus sees you and loves you as His beloved.

God makes it possible for Jews and Gentiles, men and women, masters and slaves to come together and relate to each other no longer on the basis of their society's divisions but instead on equal ground. This is possible because His love, and specifically the beloved love of God, unites people to God *and* unites them to one another. Because we are beloved to God, we become beloved to one another. And as we are beloved to one another, we will be united to one another. Professor Robert Mulholland puts it like this:

> Our relationship with God and our relationships with others are two sides of a single coin, the symbiosis of life in loving union with God for others. The place where we live out our relationship of loving union with God is not in the quiet of our prayer closet but in our relationships with one another.[2]

AN EXPANDING FIELD

Paul writes in Romans 8, "Who shall separate us from the love of Christ? Shall tribulation, or distress, or persecution, or famine, or nakedness, or danger, or sword? . . . For I am sure that neither death nor life, nor angels nor rulers, nor things present nor things to come, nor powers, nor height nor depth, nor anything else in all creation, will be able to separate us from the love of God in Christ Jesus our Lord" (vv. 35, 38–39).

To be a Christian is to be brought so close to God that you can never fall away from Him and His love. Nothing can come between you and God's love. There are no barriers, threats, difficult circumstances, current cultural tensions, or future potential problems that can separate you from God's love. Why is this? It's because to be a Christian is to be in Christ Jesus and be in the love of God. Paul describes us as being "in Christ Jesus our Lord," which means we are right in the center of God's love. We are forever rooted and secure in His love. We are always surrounded by a vast ocean of love. And nothing can take us out of it.

And it's because we all are now *in* Jesus, and *in* His love, that we then see how to love one another. We love one another in and from and with the same love in which we are rooted and secured, the same love that surrounds us and that is actually in us.

In Jesus, we are loved by God with a beloved love. So when we then turn to one another and talk about how we love one another, it will be with this same beloved love and out of this same beloved love.

Consider Paul's prayer in Ephesians 3:14–19. He prays that the church might know among themselves the love of Christ. And this happens in connection to Christ being in our hearts, which roots us and grounds us in God's love and in connection to being filled "with all the fullness of God" (v. 19). Robert L. Plummer writes, "This is what it means to live in the love of God . . . to live rationally, emotionally, and mentally in the joyful experience of Christ's love and to be transformed to reflect that love to others."[3] Scripture is rich with descriptions about being in Christ's love.

Paul tells us that God's love is "poured into our hearts through the Holy Spirit who has been given to us" (Rom. 5:5). In 2 Corinthians 5:14–20, the apostle speaks about our being controlled by the love of Christ, which then enables us to be ambassadors for Him and ministers of reconciliation. In another letter he says he yearns for the Philippian Christians "with the affection of Christ Jesus" (Phil. 1:8).

We are directly told in 1 John 4:7–9 to love one another based on the love that has been given to us from God and made us born of God and connected to God and able to live through God.

We are told to live and walk in the Spirit, and if we do so, what will come out of our being in the Spirit is love (Gal. 5:16, 22).

Similarly, in 2 Peter 1:4, as "partakers of the divine nature" we are able to embody certain qualities, among which is love (v. 7).

These passages describe God's love as being like an ever-expanding field that we are surrounded by and play within. His love is like an ever-flowing spring that seeps into every part of our souls and lives. His love is like a powerful engine that compels us to travel only on the roads of divine love.

This love that surrounds us, this love that flows through us, this love that drives us, is distinctly the love of God that we have because we are in Christ Jesus and have the Holy Spirit within us.

> **Putting on Jesus means seeing and treating people as Jesus does. And Jesus sees and treats His people as beloved.**

To be born again is to be born into Jesus. We are united to Jesus. Our former life is gone; we live out of being "hidden with Christ in God" (Col. 3:3). So when it comes to how we consider other people, relate to other people, or interact with other people, it happens out of our being in Jesus and united to Him. Being in Jesus means we "put on" Jesus in all that we do. And putting on Jesus means seeing and treating people as Jesus does. And Jesus sees and treats His people as beloved.

Here then is the key. To be united together like the Bible calls us to, we must love one another. And the strongest way for us to love one another is to see and treat others as being beloved to us. We do this because they are beloved to Jesus. By faith in God and by virtue of being born again of the Spirit of God who lives within us and fills us with divine love, we love others with His beloved love.

IN THE FULL SCOPE OF GOD'S LOVE

God is love; in and within Him is love. We by faith in Jesus are brought right into this love, to experience it and share in it. As it says in Jude 21, we are to keep ourselves "in the love of God." We remain within, we live out of, we are ruled by the love of God in Christ. First John 4:7–13 reminds us that love is from God, for God is love, and that to "abide" in God is to "abide" in His love.

If we "abide" in God, then we are kept in, or "abide" in His love. We may then live out of the fullness of His love, drawing from all dimensions of Him and His love when we relate to one another.

We abide in all aspects and dimensions of His love. We don't abide in some of His love, we abide in all of His love. For love to be perfected among us we must be connected to all of God's love.

There are so many aspects of God—more than we can comprehend—and we relate to one another out of being in all of who God is. So, for example, we abide in God as Father. Because of this, we love one another out of abiding in and being connected to the familial love of God. John speaks of loving one's brother (or sister) immediately after talking about being loved by God (1 John 4:21). We are made family by God. We relate to each other as family and love each other as family because of God's familial love for us.

All this isn't to suggest that we are to act as if we are wedded to each other. We, the church, are only wed to Jesus. But as the church we are bound to God *and* to each other.

But because we abide in all of God, we don't only abide in God as Father. We don't love one another only out of His familial love. We also abide in God as our husband. And as such, we love one another not only out of His familial love; we love one another also out of His spousal, beloved love.

God's love is perfected in us (1 John 4:12) in how we love one another. And that happens out of God abiding in us. God's perfected love among us means we are talking about the full scope of how God loves us. So to love one another in a way that perfects God's love among us means loving one another in all the ways He loves us, such as His beloved love for us.

All this isn't to suggest that we are to act as if we are wedded to each other. We, the church, are only wed to Jesus. But as the church, we are bound to God *and* to each other. This bond was attained and secured in the love of God in Christ Jesus. Which, among other things, is a beloved love.

It is then in and through His "belovedness" we become beloved to one another. The same marital love that bound us to the Lord binds us to one another and fuels our ability to be united together as one people, as His beloved bride.

The key point in all this is that we love not with our own love but with His love, namely His beloved love. A car doesn't self-generate fuel. Fuel must be put inside the car in order for it to run. So also we can't self-generate the kind of love we need to be united to one another.

HIS WELL OF LOVE

The love of God is a selfless agape love expressed most directly to us from Jesus. This selfless agape love is like that of a friend dying for his friends (John 15:13). This selfless agape love is like that of a brother dying for the sake of his brothers and sisters (Heb. 2:17). This selfless agape love is like that of a husband dying to rescue his bride (Eph. 5:25). And it is this last example of selfless agape love that especially expands and enhances the ways we can talk about how to love one another. So not only do we want to love each other with the friend love of Jesus and the brotherly love of Jesus, we also want to love one another with the beloved love of Jesus.

As John writes, "Beloved, if God so loved us, we also ought

to love one another" (1 John 4:11). We love one another entirely on the basis of how God so loved us. And how He loved us is with the selfless love of a husband giving up his very life for the sake of his bride. This is the central truth of the gospel message—that Christ came and died for our sins—and one of the best ways to describe this act of love comes in the context of marriage (Eph. 5:25). This, then, is one of the best and strongest ways by which we then "ought to love one another."

The first-century church regularly used the term "beloved" in reference to others. "Greet so and so, my beloved in the Lord" in the end of Romans. "Therefore my beloved brothers and sisters" in Corinthians and Colossians and many other places. "Don't be surprised by trials, my beloved" in 1 and 2 Peter.

It all speaks to the fact that we are beloved by God, yes—but also it's the Bible showing us how we should consider one another and how we should relate to one another. The early Christians use the term "beloved" in referring to one another because believers have been made beloved to one another by faith in Jesus. And believers remain "beloved" to one another *because* we all now abide in God and His love, and that love is the beloved love of the Lord God in Jesus Christ.

You are beloved to me because we are all beloved to God in Jesus.

Indeed, this beloved love is a love that is available to us to maintain all the ways we are together and connected to one another. In order to stay one family in Christ, we must tap not only into the familial love of God but also His beloved love. In order to remain members of one body, we must consciously draw from the beloved love of God.

There is no natural human well of love within us that we can draw from in order to love one another. That well was polluted by our sin, by our selfish desires and motives. It took the saving act of God in Jesus to remake us and put a new well of love within us from which we draw. That new well is God's love. We love one another now *because* He first moved in love toward us (1 John 4:19) and then united us to Him in that same love and then filled us with that same love. As Christopher W. Morgan puts it, "The love we give and the love we receive all ultimately flow from God's love. So what does it mean to love others? As we will see, our love flows from, tends to, reflects, and is defined by God's own love."[4]

The divine love of God was poured into us (Rom. 5:5). This is the well of love that we draw from as we now look to love one another. This is the fuel tank we use to drive us in love toward one another.[5] It's God's love that we depend on, God's love that we need, for us to be His one united people across all cultural, social, ethnic, generational barriers. This unity is possible as we abide in *all* of His love. As God's people, we are filled with *all* of His love for us. Which means, for loving one another, we have available to us, necessary to us, the most passionate, fervent, committed dimension of God's love—His marital, "beloved" love.

And because His love will always remain, we know that His love will enable us to remain united as His people now and forever.

It's worth reflecting on what it means for us to be beloved to the Lord and using such reflection as an interpretive lens for how to relate to each other as beloved in the Lord, with the result that we will be more unified in the Lord. Indeed, thinking through the lens of being beloved to one another in Christ brings out distinctive aspects of how we might love one another, how we actually "live" beloved. These aspects are what we will explore in the following chapters.

Part 2

HOW WE LIVE
BELOVED

Chapter 3

INITIATIVE

Many couples have interesting stories to tell about how and when they first met.

It's always fun to hear who exactly made the first move. Who noticed who first? Who initiated the conversation that led to them dating and eventually getting married? These early days are of course critical to everything that follows. Without initiative, there's no relationship, and without an ongoing relationship, there is no marriage.

Have you ever considered the importance of initiative? Initiative matters if a marriage is to start. Initiative continues to matter if a marriage is to thrive. Initiative will be needed when there's conflict, as someone must be willing to get the ball rolling to resolve it. Initiative will be needed to do the things that will keep the relationship healthy and strong, creative and fun. It needs someone taking the time to start conversations or set up special times together.

HE TAKES THE FIRST STEPS

What is initiative in the context of a relationship? It is the willingness to take the first steps to "move" toward another person, to choose to be in relationship with them, to preemptively choose to know them and connect to them, to continue to move in the direction of that other person. Initiative is when one person is willing to act first in relation to someone else, doing this not under coercion or begrudgingly, but willingly, out of conscious desire to be in ongoing relationship with another person.

The strongest example of initiative is with God, shown in His moving to choose, or elect, a people for Himself. Because He chooses to be in relationship with us, He takes the initial necessary steps toward us to make that possible.

We see this with Israel in the biblical storyline. God moves first toward Israel, to choose this people for Himself, to make them His "treasured possession" (Ex. 19:5). It is God who initiates and establishes the relationship.

This choosing of Israel goes all the way back to God calling Abraham and committing to specially bless him and his descendants (Gen. 12:1–3). When the Israelites are in bondage in Egypt, God initiates a plan to rescue them. He directs Moses to bring them to Himself (Ex. 19:4), out of Egypt, leading them to Sinai, where He formally recommits Himself to be in covenant relationship with Israel. The Lord then continues to lead the way, going before His people to lead them to the promised land where He will be among them, like a new husband bringing his bride home.[1]

God makes clear that the Hebrews, or Israel, did not have anything particularly special about them that they should be noticed and chosen. Compared to the other great nations they were decidedly unimpressive and unattractive. He even said, "It was not because you were more in number than any other people that the LORD set his love on you and chose you, for you were the fewest of all peoples" (Deut. 7:7). Israel has a relationship with God because God chose to love them and establish a relationship with them going back to the time of Abraham and Isaac and Jacob.

Over the ensuing centuries, Israel regularly strays from God. But He continues to take the initiative to restore and keep relationship with Israel. Seock-Tae Sohn describes how the Lord causes the earth to bring forth grain, new wine, and oil (Hos. 2:21–23) as part of the Lord's restoration of relationship with His wife, Israel. This restoration is wholly from the initiation of the Lord toward Israel, culminating in His finally restoring His people as His bride.[2]

> **God eagerly seeks His people. He is the one willing to make the first move, even when we move away from Him.**

Similarly, Matthew Haste describes the Lord's initiative, mentioned in Hosea 2:14–23, to "rekindle the broken romance" between Himself and Israel. Despite Israel's unfaithfulness, the Lord still chooses these people for His own.[3]

God does not do this begrudgingly or reluctantly. He is not forced to do it or tricked into it. Rather, God eagerly seeks His people. He is the one willing to make the first move, even when we move away from Him. He is willing to allure, indeed, dare we say seduce, them back to Himself.[4]

I still have a T-shirt I wore when I was in high school, so it's over thirty years old. It has clearly seen better days. It does not measure up to the many newer T-shirts in my closet. Yet when I go to pick out a shirt to wear late at night as I'm getting ready to relax in bed, I often look for the old, comfortable one to wear. I don't have to be told to this; I do it myself, because within me is a natural fondness for that particular shirt that I can't shake and don't want to shake. I will notice and look out for that special shirt.

There is a long history between God and His people. And when we review that history we might wonder if God should choose to be done with those who were so faithless and pick someone newer and better. Yet over and over He sticks with His people. His fondness for them causes Him to always seek them out and intentionally move toward them with committed love.

HE DRAWS TOWARD US

What was true with Israel holds true as we now think more broadly of the church as the people of God. For when it comes to having a relationship with His people, God always takes the initiative toward us, instead of the other way around. Without His taking the initiative, we would have no relationship with Him, because there was nothing in us that was even looking in God's direction. It's more accurate to say we were actively moving away from Him. Our regular tendency is to ignore, disobey, and fight back against God. Yet He still moves toward us. He still keeps calling us to Himself.

When the story is told about how God and His people came to be in relationship with each other, it will always begin with "Once upon a time, even before time began, God saw us, chose us for Himself, and moved toward us in love." The apostle John writes, "In this is love, not that we have loved God but that he loved us" (1 John 4:10). Paul notes that before the foundation of the world God chose us in love for Himself (Eph. 1:4).

Not only has God taken the initiative to pursue us and be committed to us, He was the one who first turned toward us, took our hand in His, and said the words "I love you." He is the one who was first ready and willing to be in an exclusive relationship with us. He is the one who took the needed steps to atone for our sins so that we could be in relationship with Him. Romans 5:8 reminds us that, incredibly, "God shows his love for us in that while we were still sinners, Christ died for us."

The church is made up of a people whom God actively

pursued and then drew into His loving embrace, rescuing us from the sinful darkness of our own making. Ephesians 2:13 describes us as having been "far off" from God. We were of such a distance from Him there was no possible way for *us* to find our way back on our own. Thus it took Jesus to start the journey and travel the long distance to find us and then bring us near to God "by the blood of Christ."

In John 6:44, Jesus says that no one can actually come to Him unless God "draws him." It is God who makes the first move for us to be in relationship with the Lord.

In Ephesians 2:1–8, we are described as having been dead in our sins, fully engaged in our sinful passions. And we would have remained there—for the only thing dead people can do is be dead. But God "because of the great love with which he loved us" (v. 4) takes the initiative to make us "alive together with Christ" (v. 5). He elects us in love. He does not leave us as lifeless, but sees us and pulls us into His loving embrace, wrapping us in His care and devotion, giving us new life in Christ.

This love is a familial love, in that it is the love of God the Father for us, choosing us for His own to be part of this family.

And it is also a marital or beloved love, as expressed through Jesus. That in Jesus God moves toward us with the love of the husband desiring and choosing us as His one and only bride.

CHOOSE TO DRAW TOWARD ONE ANOTHER

As God's initiating love draws us to Him, it will also draw us to one another. As Ephesians 2 makes clear, God in Christ Jesus moves toward us to bring us who were far off from Him near to Him *and* also then near to one another, such that we can be joined together to God in Christ Jesus. God's pursuit of us, His election of us, His choosing of us in love, flows to us and now flows through us to one another. We ride the momentum of God's love for us to then love one another. We move in love toward one another because God first moved in love toward us (1 John 4:19).

This does not naturally happen. In fact, our tendencies today are to move away from others rather than toward them. We expect others to take the initiative.

Think of dining at a highly rated restaurant. We don't go to a four- or five-star restaurant expecting to wipe off our table or get our own plates, utensils, and napkins, or clean up after the meal. We expect to sit down and have servers coming around to bring us what is needed and to regularly check in on us without being summoned to see how we're doing.

> **Divine love empowers us to show attention and sympathy and forgiveness, and to be willing to be the first to do that in our relationships.**

Similarly, we tend to approach relationships and community expecting that others will be the initiators. We all have legitimate needs. We all have legitimate problems and concerns, many of which are serious. And the expectation is that any community we are part of will see these needs, understand these problems and concerns, and always move toward us to care for us and help us. Of course, a church made up of people who are all doing that ends up being a community of passive pew sitters—people who are around each other but do not relate to one another because only a few take the initiative.

But initiative is fundamentally about moving toward others and doing so without expectation or need for prompting. Someone is sobbing as they sit in their seat after the worship service has ended. Initiative means you don't wonder in your mind what's going on; instead you move toward them with kindness and care.

A family with children just came through the door, clearly flustered and unsure what to do. Do they know where the nursery is, or where classes for their kids are held? Initiating love means we don't wait for them to ask; rather, we miss out on getting coffee for ourselves and settling into our favorite seat and instead take the time to help them find their way.

There's a person who's been a member for a couple of years and normally has been very involved in the church, but has recently become less involved and attending on Sundays less. We can be curious about what is going on but ultimately say and do nothing. Or instead, we can initiate by texting or phoning to learn what is going on and seeing what can be done to get them connected back into the community.

Someone is caring for an aging parent or an ill spouse and could use a few meals to be brought over. Take initiative. Don't wait to be asked. Move toward them assuming help is needed and wanting to offer help. Let God's love flow through you—individually and as a church community—into others.

We need the power of divine love to help us move toward others. Taking initiative—making the first move to establish a relationship and keep investing in the relationship—is hard for most of us. It's like a stalled car. We try to rev the engine of our heart but nothing happens. But initiative is not something we need to do or even can do on our own power. Divine love is what powers our hearts—revs the engine, so to speak—such that we can move toward others.

God's love works not because of the other person but in spite of the other person. Not every person will respond to our attempts to help or show love or take the initiative. But God's love is especially about acting toward those who, like us, could never earn and do not deserve relationship with God yet still receive it.

This initiating quality of divine love is within us by faith.

And so it is what we draw from to help us overcome passiveness and isolating habits. It empowers us to show attention and sympathy and forgiveness, and to be willing to be the first to do that in our relationships. It gives us the eyes to see everyone, especially the marginalized and overlooked. It fills us with the affection and passion to start new relationships and keep investing in existing relationships.

> **Choose to keep noticing people, paying attention to who they are and caring about their lives, and be the first to do all that is needed to mature that relationship.**

This is a different way to think about the people around you. Rather than cataloging all the reasons why you should not take initiative toward others, you, fully conscious of the reasons why they may not deserve your initiative, still have love and care for them and move toward them. Even for those who resist, the more of the Lord's love you depend on to still choose them, the more you will be able to keep pursuing them in His love.

Choose to make that phone call to someone. Choose to address a past hurt and take the initiative to work through a process of confession, repentance, and resolution. Choose to invite someone new to the community to a lunch or coffee. Choose to slow down and not rush out after a meeting but instead take the time to listen to someone share what is going on in their lives and pray for them.

In general, it is choosing to keep noticing people, paying attention to who they are and caring about their lives, choosing to be in relationship with them, and being the first to pursue them that is needed to mature that relationship.

When we are a community of "beloved" who in love initiate relationship with one another, it means more people are noticed.

It means relational problems and sins aren't ignored and brushed under the rug; rather, there is momentum to address them, there is willingness to do what's needed and keep coming back to the table until things are rightly addressed.

———

This really does mean that there is always a way for a community to come together and stay together. Taking initiative to be in relationship with others is not about one meeting. And it doesn't mean there aren't times when the relationship is stalled because more time and confession is needed to chip away at the blocks that have formed between you and the other person or persons. But taking initiative has no expiration. And it has no way of being exhausted. Especially as we see that it comes out of the endless riches of God's grace and love.

Chapter 4

WORDS

"Sticks and stones may break my bones but names will never hurt me."

Do you remember the first time you realized that this saying was complete nonsense? I suspect it was early on; perhaps a family member was shaming you for something, or maybe it was at school and the first time you got teased by a classmate. Something was said, and it hurt you in a way that you could not ignore or dismiss. Later on those words would come back to your mind, like a song you can't get out of your head, to hurt you all over again. I remember when I moved to a new school and someone made fun of my name, coming up with a demeaning way to mispronounce it. This happened over thirty-five years ago, yet I still remember what was said and still even feel a bit of how annoying and hurtful it felt.

Words can hurt us. And they can do so in ways even worse than being physically hurt. They seep into the most vulnerable parts of our souls. Certain words said to us at certain times in our lives linger in our memories and can leave emotional scars long after they were first said.

My wife, Dennae, was often told during her childhood that she was difficult, incapable, inarticulate, opinionated, and less attractive than other family members. She is well into adulthood now, a great wife and mother and competent leader in multiple spaces. Yet those words still surface in her memories. She's had to engage a lot of support and prayer to keep at bay the power of these words in her life.

"A RESTLESS EVIL"

The Bible warns us about the dangerous power of our words. James describes the tongue as "a restless evil, full of deadly poison." It is "a fire" from hell itself, "setting on fire the entire course of life" (James 3:6, 8).

Those who live in California and the Pacific Northwest know well the power of fire. Just one small spark and a few acres of forest burn to the ground. You can see the smoke from such fires blazing many miles away, even from other states.

Our words have the same destructive power. You can light a fire of words with just a small tidbit of gossip or a little innuendo: "Did you hear about so and so?" It could be a joke about someone, made in front of other people. It could be an angry response. It could be something you say that tempts people to make a decision or get involved in a situation they really should avoid. It could be unnecessary flattery or ego-stroking that props up people in power who really should not be in such a position. Or it could be criticism that erodes social bonds and trust over things that are trite and insignificant.

It can even be cloaked in piety: "Maybe I shouldn't say this, but you'll want to pray about . . ."

What's remarkable is what just a few casual comments can do. Like a spark that soon grows into a raging fire, words can corrode your sense of self, your relationships, your most basic trust in God and people and life.

BOUNDLESS OPPORTUNITIES

Of course, words can also be used to strengthen and build people up. The right words can fill our hearts with joy and goodness. Instead of destroying, they can heal; instead of cursing, they can bless. These are words being used at their best.

But many people do not experience words being used at their best. So often words are used to weaken rather than to strengthen, to demean and harm rather than to help.

With today's technology, we've never had more contexts in which to use words. Humans have progressed from early on in human history when we had our voices and writing, to having the ability to record our voices, and eventually developing the mediums of radio and then television, which allowed our words to go out to countless people, even people we have never met and will never meet. Through the internet and the cellphone, that ability has multiplied exponentially.

Yet all of these added mediums have not led to a larger increase in kinder and more gracious words filling up the world. Rather, these added opportunities have tipped the scale even more toward using our words in harmful and destructive ways. In particular, the nature of these new spaces—their online, always-on, soundbite-favoring nature—has incentivized us to find ever more creative ways to set our communities on fire with our words. They have even degraded our ability to use words well in the most basic and original medium: in our personal, face-to-face relationships with each other.

Here I'm talking not just about how we tend to use words in harmful ways. Here I'm also briefly noting our society's growing difficulty in having regular, intentional, sustained conversations with one another. We are less inclined to speak to one another directly, and on the occasions that we do, we settle for what's innocuous and superficial.

"How ya doing?"

"Good, how 'bout you?"

"Good."

"Doing anything later?"

"I don't know, hanging out I guess."

"Cool."

"Okay, see you later."

Add to that basic script perhaps some mention of a sports event or volume of work to do that week, and you have perhaps the "best" and most typical version of a modern-day in-person conversation with a coworker or classmate.

OCEANS AND DARTS

The church is subject to and beholden to these same cultural currents. Many churches are sustained by interactions that are brief and infrequent, marked largely by passing comments as we arrive (late) to a worship service and then quickly leave after said worship service. And when there are conversations, we too often default into gossip, into criticism and judgmentalism.

It's no surprise then that when there is an unsettling event—the sudden leaving of a pastor, a moral failure by a trusted leader, societal unrest, a worldwide event like a global pandemic—we struggle to have the kind of conversations that help those in the church community understand one another and stay together through the disruption.

Our ability to use lots of words in various contexts has made things worse for church relationships, not better. This makes our tendency to use hurtful and inconsiderate words in so many of these contexts all the more damaging. Brief and infrequent interactions can't keep people together when faced with a church community regularly swimming in an ocean of critical, sarcastic, hurtful, and just plain mean words.

Even more sadly, what I've seen in recent years is that even in those cases where there are many years of conversations, where the relationships among fellow believers seemed robust and solid from the many times of shared worship and meals and prayers, that even here it can only take a few words to slowly then quickly incinerate the relationships that were there.

Whether it is an ocean of critical words or just a few darts of harsh words, the poisonous, destructive power of words work, and they work well.

A few years ago, I learned that a church member had shared with someone else an unkind criticism of me. What has stuck with me is that this was a person I had worked with, one I considered a friend, close enough that they would talk with me directly if they found fault. Instead, I learned that this person was discussing their personal critical opinion of me with another person. I approached the person about the matter, and there was an apology and forgiveness. But still, things had changed between us. The person's words, perhaps just carelessly spoken, lingered and hardened in both our memories in a way that we could not easily or quickly overcome.

Among the most immediate effects of the entry of sin in our world was the deterioration of the relationship between Adam and Eve. They went from being "one flesh," naked and unashamed with each other, to covering themselves and hiding. Related to that is the change in how Adam spoke of

> **There is hope for us, however. We can reform how we use our words when we look first not to our relationships with one another but to our relationship with God.**

his wife. In Genesis 2, Eve was "bone of my bones and flesh of my flesh" to Adam. But in Genesis 3, Eve became "the woman" whom Adam blamed for his own sin. Here is the beginning of the corrosive power of words in all relationships, even our most intimate relationships. We can offer lots of tips and advice on how to speak to one another. But the sin in our own hearts will inexorably tug on us to think first of ourselves, our own benefits and desires, and to speak to one another in ways that will benefit us and satisfy our desires.

There is hope for us, however. We can reform how we use our words when we look first not to our relationships with one another but to our relationship with God. Here we find a God who has always and only used words toward us for what is true and good. A God whose words lead to relationships oriented not to selfish gain but beneficial love toward one another.

WORDS OF GOD

God spoke the first words in history. Those words were words of power and authority. God speaks, and everything is created. God speaks, and all creation listens and submits.

But among these words of power and authority were a particular set of words. Intentional words are spoken by God in regard to the human race, namely that out of all the creatures in the world, only human beings would bear His image. The first spoken words about humanity in the Bible reflect God's heightened interest in us, such that He would make us the one and only being that would be a direct reflection of Him.

Eventually God establishes a relationship with Abraham. Out of His commitment to this man, He would seek to form a people throughout human history from every nation on earth. This relationship is so committed, so close, that it is best described as being in essence a marriage between God and His people. And it's here, in this intimacy, that we see a different way to use our words. God uses His words to initiate and establish, nurture and sustain the relationship. When God intentionally speaks to us, His people, His beloved bride, we see what it looks like to speak words of love to another person.

> **We want to speak words that commit us to each other, to nurture and sustain each other. We have the ability to do this through Christ.**

God initiates and establishes a relationship with us by choosing us before the world and time itself began. Before God said "Let there be light," He was saying to His people, "I love you. I choose you. I will save you and be with you forever" (see Eph. 1:4).

As God continues in relationship with us, He regularly speaks in love to nurture and sustain this relationship with us. These words of love cement our bond with Him in a way that will outlast everything. As Lauren Winner has suggested, our baptism vows, which are in effect our marriage vows to the Lord, will outlast even our own human marriage vows.[1]

This divine relationship is the context within and the foundation for how we use our words with one another. Instead of the trends of harmful, divisive words, we want to speak words that commit us to each other, to nurture and sustain each other. We want to speak words of love to one another. What we have been given is the ability to do all this through Christ. In Jesus, we see people as Jesus does, which leads us to speak to people as Jesus does. And how does Jesus see and speak to us? As His beloved bride. This means that we now are to see and speak to each other as people beloved to Jesus. When we speak to one another as being beloved to Jesus, we counteract the forces that draw our words away from one another, that incline us to say words of harm and hurt to each other. We now speak words that initiate, establish, nurture, and sustain relationships of love that will endure and flourish.

THREE WAYS TO "SPEAK" BELOVED

What kinds of words reflect the beloved love of Christ? What might give us the most practical help? One good place to look is the Song of Songs.

We'll speak again in chapter 8 of how the human marriage spoken of in the Song of Songs reflects our divine marriage. As such, it is a window into understanding how the Lord loves us that we can reflect in our love to one another, and in this particular case, how to do so with the words we use.

Words that treat others as beloved will do the following:

Show that you really see someone

In chapter 1 of Song of Songs, the woman talks about how dark her skin color is from having worked in the fields (vv. 5–6). This makes her doubt herself, whether or not she will be desired and wanted.

And the man's response? Here is how he speaks to her:

"If you do not know, O most beautiful among women, follow in the tracks of the flock, and pasture your young goats beside the shepherds' tents. I compare you, my love, to a mare among Pharaoh's chariots. Your cheeks are lovely with ornaments, your neck with strings of jewels." (vv. 8–10)

The man reassures his future wife through his words. She is "most beautiful among women." She is "my love," to be compared to a prized horse decorated with expensive jewels.

In fact, three times in chapter 1 he calls her beautiful. And she is beautiful not because she needs society to tell her that, but because her husband acknowledges her as beautiful.

This is a theme that runs throughout the book. The man notices her. He *really* notices her. He sees her and he shows that he sees and delights in her by what he says. In 4:1 he says,

"Behold, you are beautiful, my love, behold, you are beautiful! Your eyes are doves behind your veil. Your hair is like a flock of goats leaping down the slopes . . ."

and he goes on from there. The woman offers the same kinds of words to her husband. For example, 2:8–9 says,

"The voice of my beloved! Behold, he comes, leaping over the mountains, bounding over the hills. My beloved is like a gazelle or a young stag. Behold, there he stands behind our wall . . ."

Jesus is also someone who always sees us. He is the one who sees the woman at the well and with His words acknowledges her and calls her to find relationship with Him, where she will no longer be an outcast but a beloved member of God's people. He is the one who sees Zacchaeus and invites him to spend time with Him, speaking such words over him that lead to

Because Jesus speaks words that show He sees us and notices us and cares for us as His beloved, so also in Him we speak such as to see, notice, and care for people.

this man no longer being a hated tax collector but now a beloved member of God's people.

Because Jesus speaks words that show He sees us and notices us and cares for us as His beloved, so also in Him we speak such as to see, notice, and care for people. Indeed, the most basic word that shows you see and notice someone is "hello." Love can grow among people within a church simply by that one word!

And how much more it grows if you can add other words to that one word of greeting. If for example, you remember and then regularly speak someone's name to them, it shows you care enough to remember something about them and confirms your desire to establish a relationship with them. If you notice perhaps that someone is sad or tired, love is shown when you speak words that show your care and concern for them. If you see a person who is busy and overwhelmed, you show love when you offer words of help and encouragement. If you hear about a significant and important moment, whether it's a new job, a graduation, an achievement at school, an engagement, we show love when we express words of joy and celebration with them.

Show that you honor and appreciate the other

He: "As a lily among brambles, so is my love among the young women."

She: "As an apple tree among the trees of the forest, so is my beloved among the young men. With great delight I sat in his shadow, and his fruit was sweet to my taste." (Song 2:2–3)

Here is an example of mutual praise for each other. She stands out in his eyes. She is a flower in a field of thorns and weeds. He is the one and only delight for her, the unique apple tree for her.

Their beloved is not just one of many. Their beloved is especially for them. Their words express this honor and appreciation of their unique, committed relationship with each other.

The Song of Songs several times shows the couple honoring and appreciating each other with their words.

"You are beautiful as Tirzah, my love, lovely as Jerusalem, awesome as an army with banners. . . . My dove, my perfect one, is the only one" (6:4, 9).

God also speaks words that honor us and show that we are valued by Him. As we've noted, the first words expressed by God about humanity reflect this, as God declares that out of all the creatures in the universe, including supernatural beings like angels and cherubim, human beings alone will bear His image (Gen. 1:26). There was no greater honor in all creation than that of God saying to us, "You alone are created to be like Me." Every time God speaks from that point forward there is behind His words the sense that we are valuable because we have been made in the image of God.

As God honors us, so also we honor others, out of the love God has for them that is in our hearts. We do this when we acknowledge the basic humanity of individuals, when we value and celebrate them, and especially when we do this in front of other people. Intentionally doing so has a multiplying effect as the honor we speak toward someone gets picked up and reaffirmed by others in the community.

James 2:1–7 warns against speaking toward and treating the poor among us in a way that dishonors them. This warning more positively expressed becomes an encouragement to especially speak and act in ways that show honor to the poor and others who are most often overlooked and dismissed. It is the church community that always has its eyes toward those on the outer edges of her community and then speaks and acts to create paths that lead such people toward the center, where they are noticed and valued as people who are worthy of being beloved of God and thus beloved to us.

Give blessing and affirmation to others

This is another way of looking at the opening words of the Song of Songs where the woman talks about how dark she is, and the man says, "You are beautiful." The world looks at her one way. But her husband blesses and affirms her; by his words, he redefines how she sees herself. The many physical descriptions in Song of Songs of each other's bodies are more examples of blessing and affirmation between these spouses.

Once again, let's note how from the very beginning God's words over human beings were words of love expressed in blessing. In Genesis 1:26 and 28, God blesses humanity in His command for them to be fruitful and multiply and have stewardship over the earth. This is repeated after the flood in Genesis 9, when God blesses Noah and his family and, even after this great judgment upon humanity, still blesses them with the command that they might be fruitful and fill the earth.

> The church community is a place where people can speak and receive words of blessing and affirmation.

When God speaks to Abraham, the one through whom a people would come that God would establish a special relationship of committed love, it comes in the form of a blessing. "I will make of you a great nation, and I will bless you and make your name great, so that you will be a blessing" (Gen. 12:2).

And God holds true to what He says, continuing to speak and administer blessing upon the patriarchs and His people (e.g., Gen. 35:9; Num. 6:22–27; Gal. 3:9; Eph. 1:3).

We in Christ are enabled to do the same to each other, to bless and affirm one another. As God put it to Abraham in Genesis 12:2, God speaks blessing over us so that we might speak and then be a blessing to others.

For example, our world tells so many of us that we are ugly. For some, you feel ugly because of how you look. For others, you think you're ugly because you don't have a lot of money. You may consider yourself ugly because you're not as educated as those around you. You may decide you're ugly because you are still single. You may call yourself ugly because you suffer from mental illness or mental challenges.

The church community, however, is a place where people can speak and receive words of blessing and affirmation. Words that say, "No! You aren't ugly. You are known and cared for. You are appreciated. You matter. You are deeply, intimately, passionately loved!"

One of the reasons the historic black church was a unique experience of love and unity for her members was because of how her members regularly spoke in ways to affirm and build up one another. This was a bulwark against a culture at that time that saw black people as subhuman, where an older black man would be called "boy" as opposed to "sir" or "mister." The historic black church models for us the unique power of the church to build one another up in love of God through the words we use.

All of this is not easy, for sure. We come into our relationships and into our churches already damaged by a culture full of loveless words, by personal histories where words were used to seek, kill, and destroy.

This was hellfire set loose among us. But we don't live within the gates of hell anymore. By faith in God, we live in the bosom of Jesus. And as we let His words of love to us as His beloved come into our hearts, we will heal and renew. And we will then speak and do the same to others, as His words pour through us to others around us, quenching the fire of damaging words and instead restoring and refreshing our relationships with the loving words of God.

Chapter 5

DELIGHT

Delight. It's the thrill you get during the first descent on the roller coaster you had circled on the map to go to as soon as you entered the amusement park. It's the satisfied contentment you have as you take the first bite of your favorite meal. It's the warm feeling of pleasure you get from an especially good book.

Delight is all these things. But the best and most vibrant experience of delight happens in the context of our relationships. Think about Christmas morning and that moment when the kids open up the one present they weren't expecting, the present they dreamed about having one day, what they had been hoping for. And now here it is, right in front of them. There's shock and surprise, but above all—there is delight.

This delight is initially sparked because the kids got something they really wanted. But there's more going on here than that. Delight is a response shared by both the recipients and the givers. My wife and I find joy in the giving of a great gift even as our kids find joy in receiving this gift. We are delighting in one another as we experience this moment and the thrill of opening a gift. The experience would not have been the same had the kids simply ordered their own gift online, or if Dennae and I had given them the money to go out and buy the gift themselves.

The delight is in the anticipation, the wrapping, and the opening—in sharing the moment. This is what I mean as we talk now about delight.

MEANT TO BE SHARED

Delight is a broad term that covers feelings of affection, fondness, joy, contentment, satisfaction, and thrill. However, the delight I have in mind here are all these feelings that uniquely and particularly come in the context of shared experience with someone else. Relationships arguably give us the best, most vibrant, and widest palette to experience delight. We can experience delight on our own, of course, but adding another person into the mix brings an expanded dimension of delight. I may be excited and thrilled about my new job. But to see others share this with me, to see them even get more excited and thrilled for me, broadens the initial pleasure I felt into a deeper, richer, and longer shared experience of delight with my friends.

To take this one step further, the delight we experience in our relationships is fundamentally a delight in the other person. So in the example of the gift, while the thrill of the shared experience comes as the gift is opened, what is most important is that the pleasure is being shared with a person with whom we have a close relationship. Indeed, the relationship itself brings us the broadest experiences of delight, since it is based on the person with whom we have this connection. Delight in relationship allows us to know affection, fondness, joy, contentment, and satisfaction in many forms, from the most elaborate dinner date to simply seeing this person walk into the room after having been gone a long time.

We may enjoy significant, close, and delightful relationships of many kinds during our lifetime—with siblings, friends, work colleagues, members of our church, neighbors—yet the example of marriage is unique in that a husband and wife can experience delight in every level possible for human beings: physical, emotional, intellectual, spiritual. Delight especially resonates in the context of marriage, as the ongoing union of marriage allows delight to be experienced in ever wider and deeper ways. Marriage is a context where delight can uniquely flourish.

THE DELIGHT OF THE LORD

It's remarkable then to consider that the Lord delights in us. He has joy over us, a fondness and affection for us. Our relationship to God is not purely functional, not merely efficient. God is not hanging around with us, impatiently checking His watch for when He can leave and do something more interesting. God wants to be with us, because He enjoys being with us. He simply delights in us.

He delights in us as His creation. The Bible declares it to be "very good" when humankind is created. All creation is good. But we alone get the declaration of being "very good"—a declaration of heightened delight in humanity.

He delights in us as His children. Through adoption by the Spirit we stand before God the Father alongside God the Son. By faith in the Son we stand before Him as sons and daughters of God—which means God looks at us the same way He looks at the Son: with joy and affection.

> **The Lord's desire for us is not merely that we go through the rituals of relating to Him. His desire is connected to how we know Him.**

And most especially, He delights in us as His beloved people, His bride. God has married us so that we can experience delight with Him in the widest palette possible.

Note, for example, in Hosea 6:6, how the Lord's desire for us is not merely that we go through the rituals of relating to Him. His desire is connected to how we know Him, how we commit to Him in love. His sadness and, yes, His anger is aroused when we fail to remain faithful in our love (Hos. 6:4–5). He is upset by the way we do not live up to our relationship with Him, by failing to be a people of steadfast love, justice, and righteousness (Jer. 9:24).

This is because the Lord's deep desire—His joy, His delight—is to have a committed relationship of love with us.

> His delight is not in the strength of the horse, nor
> his pleasure in the legs of a man, but the LORD takes
> pleasure in those who fear him, in those who hope in
> his steadfast love. (Ps. 147:10–11)

God's pleasure, His delight, necessitates us relating to Him with steadfast love, the kind of committed love that is tied to being in a covenantal union, i.e., marriage, with Him.

The sentiment is repeated in Micah 7:18: "Who is a God like you, pardoning iniquity and passing over transgression for the remnant of his inheritance? He does not retain his anger forever, because *he delights* in steadfast love."

The connection between delight and marriage to God is made even more explicitly in Isaiah 62:4–5:

> You shall no more be termed Forsaken, and your land
> shall no more be termed Desolate, but you shall be
> called My Delight Is in Her, and your land Married;
> for the LORD *delights* in you, and your land shall be
> married. For as a young man marries a young woman,
> so shall your sons marry you, and as the bridegroom re-
> joices over the bride, so shall your God rejoice over you.

The Lord's delight is displayed in how He has moved toward us and committed Himself to us in love. His delight comes out of loving us with the loyal love of a committed husband.

Consider the following verses, and all the ways they express God's delight:

- "The LORD your God is in your midst, a mighty one who will save; he will rejoice over you with gladness; he will quiet you by his love; he will exult over you with loud singing" (Zeph. 3:17). God can't help but sing as He is with us. When we are in trouble and in danger, He is quick to respond to help and save us. All because He delights in us.
- "They confronted me in the day of my calamity, but the LORD was my support. He brought me out into a broad place; he rescued me, because he *delighted* in me" (Ps. 18:18–19). Delight in this relationship is not a one-way street. God's enjoyment of us draws us to Him such that we too find enjoyment in Him. God delights in us, and we also delight in and find joy in Him.
- "Delight yourself in the LORD, and he will give you the desires of your heart" (Ps. 37:4).
- "May all who seek you rejoice and be glad in you! May those who love your salvation say evermore, 'God is great!'" (Ps. 70:4).
- "Then I will go to the altar of God, to God my exceeding joy, and I will praise you with the lyre, O God, my God" (Ps. 43:4).
- "Rejoice in the Lord always; again I will say, rejoice" (Phil. 4:4).

NOT JUST IN PASSING

Certainly, the history of this marriage to the Lord has not been great. God's people have done much to test and even break her bond with Him. This has made marriage to the Lord fall short of experiencing full delight.

Marriage sets up the ideal conditions for delight, but it is possible to squander the relationship and be left with an empty shell of a marriage.

I've counseled countless couples in my ministry. And I've seen far too many marriages devolve to being purely functional. The husband and wife have consigned to stay married to each other, but there is little love and certainly no delight there.

> **The Lord's affection, fondness, enjoyment, satisfaction in us, and us in Him, is our basis for having affection, fondness, enjoyment, and satisfaction in one another.**

This is how the Lord describes in the books of Hosea and Ezekiel what has happened in His marriage to His people. They cheated on Him, and thus what should have been a relationship of joy is now one of disappointment and anger.

This is why we ultimately find union with God in and through Jesus. Our betrayal of God—both the nation of Israel as related in the Old Testament and each of us as individuals—broke our relationship with Him. However, this relationship is then reforged by our faith in Jesus. Through the death of Jesus on our behalf, we are washed and made clean and remade into a people who can commit to God in Christ, and thus are able to fully delight in Him.

As we, God's beloved, delight in God, we will then, as beloved to one another, delight in each other. The Lord's affection, fondness, enjoyment, satisfaction in us, and us in Him, is our basis for having affection, fondness, enjoyment, and satisfaction in one another.

How do we do this? The simplest pathway to more delight is simply by regularly being with one another.

Joy and delight in relationship is tied to people. Our feelings of affection and fondness and enjoyment come out of being with people and sharing experiences, especially with our brothers and sisters in Christ.

"As I remember your tears," Paul writes to Timothy, "I long to see you, that I may be filled with joy" (2 Tim. 1:4). Paul will experience an overflowing amount of joy and delight if he were able to be present with Timothy again, doing life and ministry together.

Paul writes to the Romans of his eagerness to be with them. He asks them to pray that he "may be delivered from the unbelievers in Judea . . . so that by God's will I may come to you with joy and be refreshed" in their company (Rom. 15:31–32). He wants to be physically with them and enjoy the shared experience of being together that can bring them joy and delight.

Paul echoes this sentiment when he writes to the Corinthians. He hopes to stay with them while traveling through Macedonia, but he doesn't want this to be just a pit stop. He says, "For I do not want to see you now just in passing. I hope to spend some time with you" (1 Cor. 16:7).

The apostle John also expresses the pleasure of being together: "Though I have much to write to you, I would rather not use paper and ink. Instead I hope to come to you and talk face to face, so that our joy may be complete" (2 John 12). John is thankful to be able to write to them. However, the complete measure of joy and delight for John will come when he is in the presence of those reading his letter.

We need shared experiences with one another for there to be delight. My best and most delightful relationships have been the ones built upon shared experiences. In some cases, it is with people I never would have expected to have that happen.

SHARED DELIGHT IN THE LORD

In 2005, I was privileged to plant the church I currently pastor. I was a young, single, black, Baptist pastor. And my sending church partnered me with an older white businessman who had an ordination in the PCA (Presbyterian Church of America) and four kids. On paper we didn't have much in common. We had grown up differently. We had some theological differences. We were culturally not the same, except that we both were followers of Jesus. So we were both beloved to the Lord and thus beloved to one another.

And as we shared eighteen years of experience in launching and leading the church, we developed a relationship of affection and enjoyment of each other.

One of our family's favorite things to do during the summer is to hang out with Pastor Bob at his house. I smile every time Bob calls, because I always enjoy talking with him. The delight of our relationship comes out of the shared experience of being together through the death of his first spouse and his marriage to his second spouse, my marriage to Dennae, the births of kids and grandkids, the early days of financial struggles in the church plant, the joy of first baptisms in the church, and the steady work of establishing and growing a church for almost two decades of shared ministry.

Bob is among the few people in my life who I have been with through all those things, who has been there with me in Jesus, before the Lord's presence, in whom there is fullness of joy, and thus fullness of joy between us because we have been with one another in Jesus before the Lord for so long together (see Ps. 16:11).

Delight and joy are possible within the church, and it's possible when we see the value of and invest in being with one another.

Relationships of beloved love in the church prioritize interactions with one another in shared experiences. It is in those interactions and those shared experiences that delight in one another will begin to naturally grow because they will come out of the soil of our shared delight in the Lord.

The Bible studies and prayer meetings. The conversations during car rides. The debates in coffee shops. Biking and hiking together. The picnics and the sports events and the movie outings. In all of these settings, we are in Jesus together with one another, and in so being, we have the means for joy and delight in each other as we live our day-to-day lives delighting in Him and He in us.

And it gets better. In this new creation we will be with the Lord forever.

And it gets better. What we do now is meant to be a taste of what is to come. One day, all of heaven and earth will be made brand new. And this brand-new creation is designed to be a setting of delight and enjoyment. One reason this will be possible is because in the new heavens and new earth we will have restored bodies. We won't be ghostly souls, we will have bodies like we have now, but free from decay and sickness and sin. In this new creation, we will be with the Lord forever. In His actual presence. In the same space with Him. We will see Him and talk to Him directly, unmediated.

And because our bodies will be renewed, and because we will be in the same space with God, free from sin and all that has gone along with it, we will experience delight with one another and with God at way greater depths than we can right now. Yes, the food will taste better, the air we breathe be more refreshing, scents will be sweeter and colors more vibrant. All that we do together with one another before the Lord, even the most normal and basic activities like walking down the street, will delight us at deeper levels than we ever thought could be possible.

Living in bodies free from sin and living alongside other believers who are also free from sin will be a more delightful and joyful experience than anything we have ever experienced, even the greatest delights on earth.

Chapter 6

INTIMACY

Every so often I mistakenly call someone other than my wife "honey" or "babe."

It's usually when I'm talking quickly. Most often it happens with one of my kids. It just slips out. "Hey can you get the door, babe—oops, sorry, I meant Mya," or "Oh thanks, hon—oh I meant Jovanna." My kids always giggle at me with teasing outrage when this happens. "What did you just call me?" they'll mockingly ask. They of course think it's funny because clearly, while I love my kids, I don't think of them as my honey or my babe. Those terms are reserved for my wife as they reflect a particular kind of closeness I have with her and her alone. They reflect the unique relationship that I share with my wife, because you don't just call anyone honey or babe. Those terms are reserved for someone with whom you are intimate.

FINE DINING, NOT THE DOLLAR SPECIAL

What do we mean by intimacy? Intimacy is being able to be with someone, free of shame and guilt and regret. It's a uniquely close relationship where you experience safety and security and refreshment, where you can be open and vulnerable, where you have the joy of knowing and being known.

We frequently think of intimacy in the context of marriage, and rightly so. Marriage is a setting for intimacy in the most enduring and safest way, because marriage involves a lifelong commitment to one person. Intimacy flourishes in such a setting.

You can't be intimate with someone you've just met. You could share things with them about how you are feeling, reveal to them a raw story from your past, or admit a weakness, all of which would draw you closer to each other. This is intimacy in the sense that, in that one encounter, you broke down barriers and connected with this person. You could even be physically intimate with someone you just met, but none of this describes intimacy in the fullest way.

Ordering from the dollar menu does pass for eating a hamburger; but as it's from the dollar menu, it means you are not after fine dining but going for the immediate and cheap pleasure of eating. It's much different to eat a high-quality piece of meat, and to do so as part of a full dining experience at a highly rated restaurant.

The intimacy we want and benefit most from is at this highest rated level. And it only comes over time, in a long-term committed relationship. You might begin to feel safe and open with someone when you first meet them, but that can only be at an initial level. You only open up to someone, and thus can become intimate with them, as you spend time with them over many months and years—and as they prove to you at multiple times in multiple situations that they are someone you can be fully "naked" with—fully open and vulnerable, able to connect with them at every relational, emotional, spiritual level.

They demonstrate to you over and over again that your "nakedness" with them will not be used against you but instead will be precious to them and valued by them and be an occasion for them to draw closer to you and for you to draw closer to them. This is the remarkable part of Adam and Eve's relationship in Genesis 2. The Bible says that that they were "both naked and were not ashamed" (v. 25). They could be fully exposed physically, emotionally, personally, and spiritually and not feel shame from such exposure but instead know connection and intimate union with each other.

Intimacy in its ultimate expression and final end is about union. Intimacy is meant to lead us to union. Adam and Eve were naked with each other, intimate with each other, which meant they could be fully

> **Intimacy in its fullest expression is about sharing in many direct experiences with someone, good and bad, exciting and mundane, delightful and hard.**

one with each other. Intimacy is drawing near to someone, near enough that you connect with them and in a sense "merge" with them the more you reveal of yourself to them and them to you.

Here again, it's possible to settle for the superficial. You can have a union with someone that is built on one string, tuned to one note. Imagine a unity built simply on a shared hobby. There can be a real intimacy there as you share unity over love for a sports team, or over a favorite book series, or over a favorite movie genre. But this is on the low end of the spectrum. Intimacy will be quickly lost and the union will fall apart if the team moves to another city, thus leaving nothing there to bond over. Or if one of you begins to read another book series or joins a different book club. What brought you together has changed, so the reason for the previous intimate connection has disappeared.

Intimacy in its fullest expression is about showing all of who you are, in ever-increasing ways, and connecting with each other the more you share of yourself, so as to achieve a more complete union. It's about a vast network of connections forged between you and this other person, intimately uniting you to one another in not just expected ways but even in unexpected ways. It is about sharing in many direct experiences with someone, good and bad, exciting and mundane, delightful and hard. All of which—all these connections and experiences—create myriad lines of intimacy with this other person that over time unites you more to that person, indeed becomes a fundamental oneness with that other person.

BEING KNOWN

Dating my wife was great. The wedding was special. The honeymoon was A+. But now, over fifteen years into our marriage, I see that in those early shared connections and experiences, we were only still hanging out in the front yard of our relationship.

Intimacy is like a vast mansion full of countless rooms to explore and reveal multiple dimensions of ourselves, such that we are drawn to and become one with another person in ever-solidifying ways. An intimate relationship that leads to intimate union comes as we open these rooms to one another and learn to be with one another in the multiple rooms of the house of our lives.

It becomes then all the more remarkable to consider that the intimacy of human marriage, and the subsequent union that comes about in human marriage, is a reflection and signpost to the intimate relationship and forever union between God and His people.

The psalmist speaks of the goodness of being near to God (Ps. 73:28), how all his ways are intimately known by and familiar to God (Ps. 139:1, 3). The prophet Jeremiah is told that even when he was in the womb, he was known by God (Jer. 1:5).

More broadly, God speaks of His unique "knowing" of Israel in Amos 3:2 ("You only have I known of all the families of the earth"). God does not know other people in the same way He knows His own people. This knowing of Israel is akin to how a husband and wife are only uniquely known to one another.[1]

In Deuteronomy 7:6–8, God talks about how he especially "set his love" on His people. This speaks to a particular kind of commitment and affection for His people. It also speaks of His uniquely intimate relationship with Israel.

> **Idolatry is the deepest kind of betrayal, and we sense God's offense and anger. Yet God's steadfast love persists for His people.**

When God says "I am your God" and then says that Israel is not to have any other gods except Him before saying "I'm a jealous God," He is saying that He expects an exclusive, intimate relationship with Israel, one where He gives Himself to them and they give themselves to Him.[2]

This is why idol worship by Israel is such a serious matter. Worship of other gods is described in the strongest terms, equivalent to committing serial adultery in view of the whole world. The relationship between God and Israel was an intimate one; Israel following other gods was a betrayal that struck at the heart of the intimacy they had with Him. The repeated adultery of Israel constantly brought a barrier between God and His people, preventing intimacy and thus union with God.

Consider this blunt language: "I know Ephraim, and Israel is not hidden from me; for now, O Ephraim, you have played the whore; Israel is defiled. Their deeds do not permit them to return to their God. For the spirit of whoredom is within them, and they know not the LORD" (Hos. 5:3–4). Or Ezekiel 16:36, which explicitly describes the worship of "abominable idols" as "whoring." Rather than be with her husband, Yahweh, Israel has given her loyalty to the nations around them and their worship to the gods of these nations.

This is the deepest kind of betrayal, and we sense God's offense and anger. Yet God's steadfast love persists for His people. He still desires and pursues intimate union with His people. The answer to the problem of their betrayal is one He will solve Himself, which He accomplishes in Jesus. The barriers between us and God are in Jesus broken down; our sin is dealt with and atoned for, clearing the way for intimacy and an even truer union with God.

KNOWN AND LOVED

In the New Testament we see many clear expressions of how God's love allows us to be intimately known by Him, and in being known, to be united to God. This is all fully realized by faith in Jesus. Consider the intimacy of His love in these Scriptures and how that intimacy, in turn, is to be experienced by us, His people, among one another:

First Corinthians 8:3 tells us how, if we love God, we are known by God.

Paul in Galatians 4:8–9 describes how we formerly did not know God but now we know God and are known by Him.

It is encouraging that "the Lord knows those who are his" (2 Tim. 2:19), which is to say, He particularly and intimately knows His people.

The apostle John refers to his readers as "beloved," encouraging them to "love one another" because "love is from God" and to love is to know God, i.e., to have intimate knowledge and union with Him (1 John 4:7–8).

The intimate union with God in Christ is most clearly

expressed, of course, in Ephesians 5:31–32, where the one flesh intimate union of human marriage is a reference point for the intimate union between Christ and the church. Every time we take Communion we are reminded how we are in union with Christ and He in us. This is what Jesus prays and wants for His followers, that they may be "perfectly one" by being fully united in God and Christ Jesus (John 17:23). This intimate union with God becomes the basis for us to also have intimate union with one another within the church.

Our union with Jesus involved God actually re-creating our hearts so that we can know Him, so that we could really be in an exclusive relationship with God, and follow through on the things that allow that to happen. This spiritual surgery means we are now a people with hearts inclined toward intimacy and union with God (Jer. 31:33) and, as a result of what we have with God, intimacy and union with one another.

> **We don't just associate with one another as believers. We are intimately one with each other by virtue of the intimate unity we have with God in Jesus . . . as "beloved."**

Multiple times in the Bible we see a call for unity, for oneness (e.g., John 17; 1 Cor. 12; Eph. 4). But what fuels and sustains this oneness is that we are united first to God in a spiritual marriage. As we draw close to God, to be one with Him, and thus intimate with Him, we also draw close to one another, to be one with one another, and thus intimate with each other.

The church does not exist, indeed cannot exist, apart from having been intimately united to God. We don't simply associate with God, we are intimately one with God. So we don't just associate with one another as believers. We are intimately one with each other by virtue of the intimate unity we have with God in Jesus.

THE KEY: BELOVED

One word that especially points to the intimate relationship, the deep connection and union among believers, is a word we referenced earlier and throughout: "beloved."

When Paul talks about his fellow Christians as he closes some of his letters, he will call them "beloved." At the end of Romans, for example, he says: "Greet Ampliatus my beloved in the Lord." "Greet Urbanus, our fellow worker in Christ, and my beloved Stachys." "Greet the beloved Persis." Similar language is found in the end of Colossians. In 1 John and 3 John, the author repeatedly refers to his readers as "beloved."

There is more behind this word than just that we are beloved in terms of being family to each other or that we are beloved in terms of being fellow citizens, though it certainly includes that. Ampliatus and Urbanus and Stachys are beloved family to Paul, and they are beloved citizens of the kingdom of God with Paul. But that does not exhaust all that is behind that word. Beloved is a term of affection and endearment. It is a marker of intimacy. The church is not made up of Christians who are biologically related to one another or legally connected to each other. Yet the Bible uses an especially strong term of relation and connection to describe our relationships with one another. It's a marker of the intimacy and close connection and union we have with one another. Referring to one another as beloved, when viewed in light of the whole biblical story, is an expression that for certain includes the intimate union we have with the Lord and thus the intimate union we have with one another.

The "one flesh" union we have with Christ means we are close to Christ and, by simple spiritual geography, we are close to one another.

Jesus prays in John 17:21 "that they may also be one *in* us."

The unity Jesus prays that we have with one another comes because we are in God, one with him, indeed intimately one. Oneness with one another happens by virtue of our oneness in God.

Intimate union within the church is not something that is often talked about. It can feel strange to even talk about being "intimate" with one another. This is mostly because our culture can only think of intimacy in terms of the physical.

But intimacy is more than that. It has to be. As we noted earlier, our intimacy with God is not a physical one, but one born in spirit since God is spirit. So we are automatically talking about a relationship of a different nature when we talk about an intimate union that is based in our union with God.

But for sure, we are talking about a relationship of real importance and significance. This is not an abstract concept. Since God is spirit and spirit is eternal, we are talking about an intimacy and union that will endure past even the best human marriages, that involves a bond and connection that will flourish way past any earthly relationship.

This is the basis by which we can be with fellow believers, indeed intimate with one another, in a way that is holy and glorious and ultimately everlasting.

"WE" AND "THEY"

Our family moved to a new home in an entirely new town after my third grade year, so I started fourth grade in a new home and a new school. I remember those first few days of class, being in a setting where I was distinctly the new kid, outside the community of friendships that the other kids had formed over the last few years. I remember how eagerly I jumped on any opportunity to "break in," so I joined a fan club for an animated series one of my classmates headed up. I also remember how happy I was to begin doing sports and do well enough to get some credibility from my new classmates. I was looking for any way that might allow me to no longer be an "other" to my fellow pupils, but someone who was part of the group, known and accepted.

Sociologists refer to this as in-group/out-group behavior. We have a natural tendency to form and be part of an "in-group" that defines itself apart from those who are outside that group. There is a "we" and a "they" and in large measure the "we" finds meaning and purpose by always having a "they" who is outside the "we."

God's love for us as His bride breaks this dynamic. For God unites Himself to us, creating only a "we" between Him and anyone who has united him- or herself to God in Christ.

This beloved love of God that unites us to Him unites us to one another such that there can no longer be a "they" or an "other" for the church. God creates a new space within us that allows us to receive others into our very selves. To invite them into our inner spaces of thought and emotion and soul. And to embrace them there.

What does this intimacy look like more specifically? Intimacy is oneness communally, emotionally, physically.

Our spiritual union is expressed in communal intimacy

Intimacy is fostered in shared space doing things together with one another. Corporate worship then is an inherently intimate act, a regular "bonding" agent for the church. Because we are all in Christ, all with the same Spirit, there is a kind of resonance when we pray together, read Scripture together, take Communion together, sing together. Worshiping together is an intimate, collective experience. Granted, in some cases we have done a lot to take the intimacy out of worship, to make it largely soulless and a production.

Worship increasingly is thought of and promoted as a primarily individualistic experience. Corporate worship, however, is not about perfunctory acts or aligning with each member's personal worship music playlist. Corporate worship at its best involves intentional unifying engagement with one another before God. In Acts 2:42–44, the early church had a shared life of worship ("And they devoted themselves to the apostles' teaching and the fellowship, to the breaking of bread and the prayers") that led to an uncommon connection to each other ("And all who believed were together and had all things in common"). Acts 4:23–31 tells of the the church's prayer meetings that strengthened their unity in the Spirit and proclamation of the Word of God.

The regular practice of Communion is one of the more direct ways we remind ourselves of and participate in intimate union with God and with one another. Every time we take Communion, we affirm how fully "in" Christ we all are and how much Christ is "in" all of us. "The cup of blessing that we bless, is it not *a participation* in the blood of Christ? The bread that we break, is it not *a participation* in the body of Christ?" (1 Cor. 10:16). This is partly why Paul emphasized several times in 1 Corinthians 11 that the Corinthians should not take Communion as separate groups (as was happening in their church), but rather they needed to intentionally come together as an entire community so that they might then take the Lord's Supper as one.

Our spiritual union is expressed in emotional intimacy

An emotive element is involved in our being beloved to one another. We must reclaim emotions as crucial to having intimacy in our relationships.

Emotional expression is a form of "nakedness" that can be more vulnerable and revealing than even physical nakedness. It's no surprise then that emotional expression in our relationships is an important basis for intimacy and union. In the same way the Lord rejoices over us or weeps with us, so also we in Christ experience the holy glory of intimacy and the blessing of union through how we empathize and sympathize emotionally with each other. As we know the freedom to laugh and cry, to lament, to rejoice, we are naturally drawn to one another and connect more deeply with one another.

Paul describes his ministry to the Lord within the church as one of "all humility and with tears" (Acts 20:19). He explains in 1 Corinthians 12 how our intimate union with one another—expressed here as being "one body"—is shown in how we express care for another, or feel the suffering of one another, or share in the joy of one another (1 Cor. 12:25–26). To be in community with one another means we "rejoice with those who rejoice, weep with those who weep" (Rom. 12:15).

All of this comes out of and supports our intimate union, which is realized because of an intimate union to God by faith in Jesus.

Our spiritual union is also expressed in a kind of physical intimacy

Here we are talking about physical presence. Presence is an important enough topic to be explored more fully in the following chapter on its own. But for now, we note the importance of presence here for intimacy in relationship. The promise of the Lord is that He is with us, and will be with us always. So also with one another, intimacy comes out of a commitment to regularly be with one another and to stay in ongoing community together.

We know from Acts 2:42–47 how much the early Christians were with each other: "Day by day, attending the temple together and breaking bread in their homes" (v. 46). Paul in his farewell to the Ephesians' elders starts off by reminding them how much time he spent in person with them: "How I did not shrink from declaring to you anything that was profitable, and teaching you in public and from house to house" (Acts 20:20). John notes that there is a deeper, more intimate joy that is only possible through him talking with his fellow believers "face to face" (2 John 1:12).

> The church today needs to make the intentional effort to physically be with one another . . . regularly being in the same spaces, at the same times, side by side, face to face.

In the early church, intimacy came out of various divergent racial and social groups—the wealthy, the poor, the master, the slave, the Jew, the Gentile—coming together to sit near one another and pass food to one another and share meals with one another. For example, Jews traditionally saw Gentiles as unclean, irreligious pagans. Gentiles considered Jews to be strange and religiously aloof. Yet in Christ they became members of the same community. This meant regularly sitting together in the same house churches, taking Communion together from the same bread and cup, sitting at the same table and passing food to one another in table fellowship. It was certainly initially uncomfortable to do this kind of cross-cultural table fellowship, so much so that even Peter briefly stopped eating with Gentiles until being rebuked by Paul (Gal. 2:11–14). But it was an absolutely necessary physical way to affirm the spiritual reality that in Christ they were one with God and now one, intimately one, with one another.

Sharing the Lord's Supper and fellowshiping together in this way meant that people who normally would be divided outside of their lives in the church now shared in a kind of "sweaty, intimate, flesh and blood embrace" that marked their fundamental unity with one another.[3]

The church today needs to make the intentional effort to physically be with one another so that we might love one another more intimately. This means regularly being in the same spaces, at the same times, side by side, face to face. It means practices of Communion together and table fellowship together.

We can go one step further than this. And that is to consider reclaiming physical touch as a way to love and unite with one another more intimately.

Touch is an important relational expression in many cultures, often expressed in the form of a light kiss on the cheek. I had to do this a lot growing up in a Haitian family. Whenever I visited my extended family, my mom would remind me and my sister that as soon as we entered the room, we needed to greet all the female members who were present there with a light kiss on the cheek. Whenever I balked at this, my mom was quick to remind me that to not do so would be highly disrespectful. And it would get me in big trouble with Mom, which was plenty of motivation for me to stop objecting and do as I was told. Looking back now, however, I see how this physical expression was an important way in our family's culture for us to affirm close connection and intimacy.

> **Touch was a key way Jesus would engage with people. Those who were most ostracized, most overlooked, most untouched, Jesus especially noticed and drew near to.**

We note as well all the ways Jesus touched others or allowed them to touch him. Jesus was in a "low-contact" culture.[4] Any upstanding Jew dare not be near certain kinds of people, much less touch them. But with Jesus, touch was a key way He would engage with people. The sick. Children. The blind. Women. Those who were most ostracized, most overlooked, most untouched,

Jesus especially noticed and drew near to them. He specifically showed His love and care for them by touching them.

Jesus could always heal with but a word from many miles away. But it's striking how regularly He heals when people come to Him, that is to say when they are in His physical presence, and how He would do His healing by actually touching people.

Touch remains an important expression of intimacy in the church, and the practice that especially highlights this is the "holy kiss." Many times in his letters, Paul will tell his readers to greet one another with a holy kiss. This would have been a light kiss on the cheek, similar to what I experienced growing up in a Haitian family, or what is done in many cultures around the world today. The holy kiss was a kind of intimacy that would have drawn Jew and Gentile closer to each other than they would ever have been or ever wanted to be. The holy kiss, however, was a marker that expressed the fact that they were united together to Christ and thus united together to one another. One of the most tragic and evil revelations in today's American church has been the exposure of so much abuse within the church.

Misuse and abuse of touch is a concern, for sure. Many have been abused by touch in terrible, lifelong-damaging ways, and certainly this misuse is never something God intended or sanctioned. But knowing God's gift of touch has been distorted in some cases should make us all the more eager to redeem touch, to have touch be the "holy kiss" that affirms our union with one another in Christ.

How might we touch in ways that are holy? Communities in different cultural contexts will have to work this out as this is not a one-size-fits-all. And some people may be rightly limited because of past abuse. But there are affirming ways to practice touch. The holding of hands with one another during prayer. The quick hug of greeting. The longer hug of care with those you have already cultivated a safe and healthy relationship with. The affirming pat on the back to congratulate or encourage someone. The hand on the shoulder as you pray for someone. The shoulder for a grief-stricken friend to cry on.

Intimacy is a risk. To invite someone to be close to you, to receive them not just into your life but into your heart, and to then allow yourself to be received into their heart, can feel like a risk not worth taking. And arguably, it's not worth the risk, given human failings and weaknesses and sinful habits and abuses. This is why intimacy like this only has a chance when we base our efforts in Jesus, who already had perfect intimate union within the Trinity, yet took the eternal risk to open up space within Himself for us to be received into Him and Him to be received into us. Swiss theologian Hans Urs von Balthasar beautifully expresses this truth:

> Here it is God, the Eternal, the Wholly Other, he who
> has no need whatsoever of creaturely love, who owes
> this intimacy to none of his creatures, who opens
> himself and gives himself to us. He gives himself to us
> by inviting us, lifting us up and ennobling us so that we
> may participate in his own divine nature.[5]

The more we see ourselves in Christ, and the more we let the Spirit fill all the parts of our heart and soul, the more space is created for a powerful, holy intimacy among believers. The soil of intimacy is tilled by God's intimate union with us. His beloved love is planted within that soil. We have only to live there with one another, and the fruit of intimate love and unity will naturally be harvested.

Chapter 7

PRESENCE

It really hit me when I opened my closet and saw it half full of women's clothes.

I was only a week or two away from getting married and Dennae had begun moving her things in. I had lived for many years as a single man. Now I was getting married and, while I understood that meant big changes, seeing another person's things in my home concretely embodied the new life I would be living. I was no longer alone, living on my own. Someone else would be present at home and I would be present with her, and all of what that included—her laughing and her crying, her conversations with me, the habits she has in the morning, her toothbrush in the bathroom and her clothes in my, now our, closet. I would be present with her for all of them since I now would live with her. And of course, all of me—all of how I live—would be with her. We would be present to each other, be with each other, from that point forward.

It is the most basic part of being married, living with one another. Your spouse becomes the person with whom you occupy the same physical space more than with anyone else.

To be beloved to someone, to commit to them exclusively in marriage, means you will be *with* them. You will talk with them.

You will do things together with them. You will have meals with them. You will sleep next to them. This is someone who will occupy the same points in time and space with you in a way that no one else will. (And in a good marriage, this will be something enjoyable and refreshing.) Their presence will shape and guide your sense of yourself and the trajectory of your life for as long as you are together.

This presence also happens to be a promise the Lord makes to us: that He is with us, and will be with us, living with us always.

BEGINNING TOGETHER

God's preferred way of relating to humanity is that He wants us to live with Him and He with us. To always be present with us and among us. Think of God with Adam and Eve in Eden, where the Bible describes Him walking in the garden. God is spirit, yet He made Himself present there in such a way that Adam and Eve could hear Him walking. This seems to have been a normal practice for Him, to be there, present with humanity, living in the home He created for us.

God "is pictured not as the King seated up on the heavenly throne . . . but as One who is very much here on earth in the garden walking and talking with his people,"[1] write Duvall and Hays in *God's Relational Presence*. This truth makes the sin of Adam and Eve all the more tragic, as their disobedience leads them not to *seek* the presence of God but to *hide* from His presence (Gen. 3:8). Their sin violated the home they had with God. Being present with God, rather than being an experience of joy and rest, now was one of shame and guilt.

The continuing biblical account shows God seeking to be with us, looking for ways to still be present with us. We will see this in the story of Israel. Over and over again, Israel dishonors

God and ignores His presence among them, going so far as to cheat on God right in front of Him by bringing idols into the land, the home they were supposed to share exclusively with God.

Yet the Lord God still wants to live with them. He is the Husband who still wants to find a way to make a home with His wayward wife.

DWELLING TOGETHER

God being married to His people automatically meant He would live with His people.[2] This was His intention from the moment He saved His people out of Egypt and committed Himself to them at Mount Sinai. He would be with them fully—and they would intellectually know and emotionally and physically experience His presence among them.

In Israel's travels through the wilderness, God's presence was represented as a cloud by day and a pillar of fire by night. His presence with them was solidified when they built the tabernacle and placed it in the middle of their camp, and then eventually the temple, which was built in the capital city.

The cloud and fire. The tabernacle. The temple. All physical expressions of the spiritual reality that the Lord and Israel were living together in the same way a newly wedded couple lives together in their first home. Seock-Tae Sohn writes, "A man and woman dwell together after marriage; likewise, Yahweh dwells among his people."[3]

But what does it really mean to say that God dwells with His people? God is spirit. He is omnipresent. He doesn't physically inhabit space and time like we do. Yet when it comes to His people, God, in a mysterious yet wondrous way, positions Himself to be with His people in a way that is unique to them and them alone. He will inhabit space with them such that they can legitimately say that the Lord dwells with them, that He is present with them. We can truly say that God and His people share a home together. He says,

> "I will dwell among the people of Israel and will be their God. And they shall know that I am the LORD their God, who brought them out of the land of Egypt that I might dwell among them. I am the LORD their God." (Ex. 29:45–46)

God wants Israel to know that He is their God, and that this is demonstrated by His "dwelling" with His people. God specifically pursued a relationship with Israel, going into enemy territory to rescue them from slavery, marry them at Sinai, and then live in the same place with His people from that point forward.

He regularly reminds Israel that as they enter into the promised land that they will do so with Him at their side. He won't leave or abandon them; instead, He will go with them into the land, because His intention is to live among them, to be with them (Deut. 31:6, 8).

TABERNACLE WITHIN

Human sinfulness complicates God's efforts to establish ongoing life with human beings. You can't live with someone who constantly insists on their own way, who is unwilling to heed the voice of their spouse. And while God dwelt with His people via the tabernacle and then the temple, even that was far from ideal. It was a highly confined kind of living. Our sin and God's holiness prevented us from more directly and fully living with God. Only the high priest could come into the presence of God, and then only behind a curtain and after sacrifices and washings.

Fortunately, this living arrangement was only ever a half measure and one meant specifically to lead the way to a more definitive answer. The incarnation was God's definitive answer to the problem. Jesus is Immanuel, God with us (Matt. 1:23). And He is "God with us" more directly than was possible before. Jesus removes the stain of our sin, cleansing us of our guilt and shame. He remakes and remodels our hearts. Our soul becomes a place in which God the Spirit lives. By faith we are in Jesus, which means God is now living *in* us. The tabernacle or the temple as a structure is no longer needed; He tabernacles within us.

This means in the best moments of your life, God is there celebrating with you and rejoicing with you. It means in the lowest moments of your life, God is also there, to encourage and comfort you. God will never slam the door and walk out of your life. He will never live in a separate bedroom of the house. God lives with us and in us and will always live with us and in us.

The best relationships are built on shared experiences and moments. One of the reasons my wife is the one person I am closest to in this world is because she is the one with whom I share the most number of experiences and moments. This has been the natural result of us living with one another, of our regularly being in each other's presence. What we have with God then is a life together with Him that will naturally grow in closeness and intimacy, because we now live with Him, having shared experiences and moments with Jesus that start the moment we believe and that will continue into eternity.

God intends to one day re-create heaven and earth such that they essentially "merge" and we can talk about being with God and God walking around with us as it was in the beginning.

For the life we have with God now on earth is only the beginning of what God is setting up for our life together. God intends to one day re-create heaven and earth such that they essentially "merge," and we can talk about being with God, and God walking around with us as it was in the beginning. And this time, it will stick. There will no longer be any threat to this living arrangement. We will live with God and enjoy a life together with him forever as John describes in Revelation 21:2–3:

> And I saw the holy city, new Jerusalem, coming down
> out of heaven from God, prepared as a bride adorned for
> her husband. And I heard a loud voice from the throne
> saying, "Behold, the dwelling place of God is with man.
> He will dwell with them, and they will be his people, and
> God himself will be with them as their God."

When Jesus says that in His Father's house there are many rooms and that He is going there to "prepare a place for you" that He might "welcome in you into My presence, so that you also may be where I am" (John 14:2–3[4]), He is stating His intention, His desire, to live with us. And even during His time on earth, Jesus could have come and done a few training sessions with His disciples, telling them what they needed to know to eventually go out and "make disciples of all nations." It certainly would have been an efficient use of time. Instead, Jesus came and lived with His disciples. He was present with them, in multiple places and settings. He walked to different places with them, ate food in the same rooms and at the same tables with them, slept in the same homes with them. What He wanted them to know came out of years of being together with them.

We will be in the same space with God forever. We will never wonder where God is because He will always be there. We will have an eternity of experiences with Him. We will tell endless stories, share countless memories of talking with God, walking with God, enjoying the new heaven and new earth with God.

This is coming one day. But as has been mentioned, we already have stepped into this reality by way of Jesus, through the Holy Spirit. We can say now that we live with God, with the promise that we will be with Him forever in the home He is already preparing for us.

PRESENT WITH ONE ANOTHER

God, by His Spirit, is among us, in our midst. We don't relate to God as if He were on stage and we were in the audience watching Him perform. Rather, God is right here with us, His presence beside us and among us. His presence in us. And to be aware of Him beside us and among us means being aware of each other. As we look at God beside us we are looking at each other. Every time we face God, we face one another. God being present with us is being present to each other. To live with God is to live with one another.

Being present with God because of His marriage commitment to us automatically means we are being present with one another. The Lord's presence with us connects us to each other spiritually but also in practical ways. So how might we embody and cultivate presence with one another as part of our ongoing presence with the Lord?

Most directly, this means we have to be in the same spaces together. We mentioned earlier the importance of corporate worship. But more broadly, this speaks to the need for believers to regularly do things together and experience things together. We will love one another with the intimacy and vitality that the Lord loves us by making sure we are regularly and intentionally *with* one another.

The early church wasn't just people sitting in worship services. The early church was also their meals together (called love feasts and seen as a natural extension of their worship). It was their prayer meetings together. The church operating out of the home context meant being present in various arrangements and many occasions. It allowed slaves to interact with and live together on equal terms with masters. For Jews to interact with and live with the "impure" Gentiles, and Gentiles to interact with and live with the religiously stuck-up Jews. It allowed high-level officials to interact with and live with day workers.

INTENTIONALLY PRESENT TOGETHER

However, the early Christians weren't perfect. One problem Paul had with the Corinthian church in 1 Corinthians 11:17–34 was that they were doing church apart rather than together. Several times Paul talks about the church coming together, and how they had allowed themselves to do their love feast and partake in the Lord's Supper apart from one another.

Upper-class Christians were arriving early and either eating ahead of lower-class Christians or eating separate from them in a private dining room. They would have been lying on their sides on nice couches, eating whole banquets of their own food, getting drunk on wine. Lower-class Christians would arrive later, resorting to eating together in the courtyard of the house church. Many of them would have had to stand because there would not be enough seats. Many would go hungry because they couldn't afford to have much food and wine.

Paul couldn't be stronger in rebuking this. He said their worship gatherings were doing more harm than good (v. 17). They were despising the church of God and humiliating their fellow Christians (v. 22).

This was a failure of presence. Relationships were being damaged because they did not wait for each other, but were participating in the Lord's Supper separately. When Paul talks about the church coming together (vv. 17, 18, 20, 33, 34) he is literally saying, "Make sure you are in the same space, at the same time, experiencing the same thing together."

Paul makes an even stronger critique of not being with one another when he rebukes Peter in Galatians 2 because he drew back and "separated himself," since he was afraid of the circumcision party (Gal. 2:12). Paul actually says that what Peter was doing was "not in step with the truth of the gospel" (v. 14).

Paul sees this as way more serious than just skipping a few meals with the Gentile Christians. It was an "othering" of the Gentile Christians by Peter and the other Jews who followed his example.

Paul is calling Peter to treat these believers not as separate but as beloved to him, because both Jew and Gentile have been brought together in the same gospel of grace by faith alone. This gospel has made them forever beloved to the Lord. And so if we are beloved to the Lord, we are beloved to one another, and our practices, like eating with one another, must reflect that. Scot McKnight writes,

> For Paul, love is central. It was central because he knew the challenge of the Christian life for those who were in fellowship with one another in house churches dotting the Roman Empire. The *only* way they would make it is if each person learned to love the others. Roman slaves and workshop owners were not used to sitting down at table and praying with Torah-observant Jews, and kosher Jews were not used to reading Scripture with prostitutes or migrant workers—yet Paul believed this

was God's greatest vision for living! Which brings us back to the need to love one another.[5]

Love within the church, if it is marked by us being beloved to another, means we cannot give up the habit of being together (Heb. 10:25). Our relationships with one another depend on being present with each other, namely by being sure to be together at multiple times in the same spaces.

We have challenges and limits in the modern era. Cars allow us to be far from one another. Work schedules for parents and sports schedules for kids mean we have a lot more going on every day of the week. We remember all the months during the pandemic when we were largely apart from one another. Social media may give the illusion of closeness, but togetherness in cyberspace isn't the same as face-to-face interaction.

God is present among believers in a unique way when we are together at the same time.

These are all challenges to be sure. And they must be consciously recognized and then actively resisted. We need to fight hard against disembodied relationships, where we have little to no in-person, face-to-face relating. This includes even those cases where we are in the same space, but we are not really *with* each other as we are distracted by our phones, the television, or endless household errands.

There is no other way around this—for us to be beloved to God we must be beloved to one another, and that requires our presence with one another. It requires reacting to the physical cues of someone, responding to what they say or don't say, sensing how people are feeling and how they are doing spiritually because we are in the same place with each other. There are ways the Lord speaks to us and gives us His grace and wisdom and love that cannot happen unless we are regularly physically present with one another.

God is present among believers in a unique way when we are together at the same time. As we orient ourselves to God in worship each week, we orient ourselves to one another. As God unites us to Himself even more to shared life together through worship, so also we become united together, seeing how we in the Lord share life together.

We must plan time to be together in worship. We may even need to find ways to make it easier to be together through the times we pick and the places we live. One of the many strong elements of the black church tradition is the priority placed on Sunday corporate worship, and in particular, the unique blessing of being there with other people. This tradition rightly affirms that there is a joy, an affirmation, a blessing, indeed a beloved-ness, that only comes from "doing church" together.

Shared worship together is like the accelerant that leads to a web of life together. I've seen it look like women in our church taking daily walks to be with other women. Or my wife going grocery shopping with other people, using that errand inten-tionally to connect with others. It's being with one another at kids' football games and graduation celebrations. It's prayer meetings and Bible studies and Friday night hangouts and after Sunday worship lunches together. It's the time spent holding someone's new baby and sharing in the joy of new life. It's the time spent mourning with someone over a miscarriage or loss of a parent or a spouse.

"CHURCH FOOD"

One of the best ways for us to be present with each other is to prioritize sharing meals together. The love feast was a common feature of the early church. Eating together is not just a thing to do and get over with. The practice of eating together means we are forced to slow down enough to be in the same space with one another, affirming our dependence on God for this food and, in sharing meals with one another, our dependence on one another. It affords time to linger with one another as you take extra time to talk and hear from each other. This is what turns the meal into a love feast—when we do so consciously with fellow believers.

In *Making Room*, her book on hospitality, Christine Pohl cites this quote: "In a world of hatred and conflict, with its racism and deprivations, the saints are able to sit together at their welcome tables and remind one another in the giving and receiving of food, that they may continue to believe that 'the greatest of these is love.' There is nothing like church food."[6]

A special mention should be made here about the underrated but essential Christian practice of hospitality. Regularly being with each other in one another's homes is a tangible way we "live" with one another and are present with each other. It is a direct way we can be beloved to one another as it requires a welcoming of someone into your inner life. The direct biblical commands to show hospitality to another within the church (Rom. 12:13; 1 Peter 4:9) are practical expressions of the Lord's hospitality to us, which is itself born out of His desire to be with us as much as possible. We welcome one another, to live with one another with love and affection, based out of how the Lord welcomed us, who did so with love and affection for us (Rom. 15:7).

Hospitality is also one of the more visible means by which the Lord's love for those on the margins and who are among the most ignored and dismissed by society is expressed. When we "live" with those who are considered "the least" in our world, we are loving them and demonstrating that they are worthy of being loved. This is true because God loves them. He loves them enough to invite them to be His bride just like anyone else. Hospitality to the sinners, the marginalized, the overlooked, the ignored, and the frowned upon is a direct way we demonstrate that this love of God is true also for them.

And we do all these things not just to do them, but because we are meant to live together by virtue of being beloved to the Lord and thus beloved to one another. So if we are meant to be together, we should be together!

Some of the most important and even difficult conversations can only happen when we are together in multiple spaces, in multiple settings. Discussions on race and politics often become difficult and tangled because they happen in a void. They are happening between people who never really have been with each other. These discussions, while still difficult, are much less tangled when they occur between people who regularly "live" with each other through both formal church services and informal settings. These discussions need more space to roam than one conversation or event can provide. And fortunately, they find that space among people who can allow such discussions to occur in the broad range of settings they already have, and continue to have, in their life together.

Making time and space to be with one another, and to be willing to do it a lot, is one of the most loving gifts we can give to one another because our time and presence is one of the few things in this world that are not renewable. If you run out of money, you can work more and get more money. If you run out of food, you can go out and get more food. But once today ends, that day is forever gone. You can't go out tomorrow and get another day like the day you are living right now. The time you spent today and how you experienced that time is spent and then gone forever.

We all have only a certain number of Sundays, Mondays, Tuesdays, and all the other days of the weeks within us. What a precious thing it is then to share this wonderful, irreplaceable resource with someone else: the gift of your time and your presence, to really be with each other in ways that say, "You are not a thing. You are a person. And in Christ, you are even more. You are beloved to me in Christ, and so I freely and generously love you with my time and my presence."

Chapter 8

COMMITMENT

Why do a marriage ceremony in front of people? Do you need an audience in order to get married?

Technically, no. You can get married at a courthouse in front of a judge. You could arrange a private ceremony in your backyard with just you, your partner, and the officiant. There are even ways to get married online. You will be legally married if you use any of these options.

But there is something significant about getting married in front of a group of people, especially in front of your community. A marriage ceremony in front of others means you are saying publicly, "I am committed to this specific person. You all bear witness to this and hold me accountable to be in an exclusive relationship with this person." A public ceremony reinforces a fact that is true for all marriages, no matter how they are done—namely, that marriage is a promise to uniquely and exclusively commit yourself to another person.

Some relationships can end simply by breaking a lease. Some relationships will go away if you merely unfollow these individuals and delete their photos from your phone. Other relationships start to fade away the moment you change jobs, or gyms, or churches.

But marriage is different. It means I am willing to be tied to this person in a way that matters, where I will be bonded to this person, where I am willing to thoroughly entangle my life with this person. It won't be as easy to immediately remove yourself from this person's life, especially the longer you have been married to them.

You have and will have lots of relationships in your life. But in marriage, you promise to hold this relationship with your spouse as the one you will exclusively commit yourself to above all other relationships.

EXCLUSIVE COMMITMENT

The relationship of God with His people is this way. It is based on the premise of monogamy—exclusive commitment. We are in an exclusive, committed relationship with the Lord. He belongs to us, and we belong to Him.

Marriage in the ancient Near East was often expressed as a kind of owning, where the husband "owned" his wife. He was in possession of his bride. We of course don't talk this way today, for good reason. But we can appreciate how this language is co-opted by the Bible to strongly say that Yahweh and His people are in a committed relationship. So we see God speaking of owning Israel, that Israel is His own special possession.[1]

> As we declare that the Lord is our God, we at the same time are then made His people, and as such bonded together by His word to us.

However, God is not viewing Israel like a prized heifer that He owns, as if the people were simply a product or commodity to Him. They are a *special* possession to Him—special because His "owning" them expresses His commitment to them. A commitment to specifically set His love and attention on them.

So in Exodus 19:5, God speaks of Israel as "my treasured possession among all peoples."

In Deuteronomy 7:6, God again speaks of Israel as His "treasured possession, out of all the peoples who are on the face of the earth," going on to add that He did not commit to specially "set his love" on them because of how great a people they were, but simply because He chose to love them and keep the commitment to specially love them that He made to their forefathers. So also in Deuteronomy 26:18–19, the Lord declares Israel to be "his treasured possession," a people "holy to the LORD," who the Lord will set "in praise and in fame and in honor high above all nations that he has made." God speaks of how He chose Israel and will not reject the nation (see Isa. 41:8–9). He will instead remain committed to a relationship with Israel.

As we declare that the Lord is our God, that we are committed to Him, we at the same time are then made His people, set apart specifically for Him, and as such bonded together by His word to us (revealed to us today in and through Jesus) so that we can faithfully be His people as described in Deuteronomy 26:17–19.

God declaring that "You are my people" and their responding "You are my God" (see Hos. 2:23) is a slight variation of the marriage declaration "You are my wife, you are my husband."[2]

The Song of Songs is a book we have already mentioned as being not only about human marital love, but an allegory of the love relationship between God and His people. Song of Songs repeats the phrase "I am my beloved's and my beloved is mine." We see a sense of possession here. In other contexts, this would be strange and off-putting. You don't want a boss telling his employees, "You are mine!" But in the context of marriage, this statement of possession is an expression of unique, exclusive commitment to each other. You are mine, and I am yours, and we belong to no one else but each other. We are each committed to the other, and thus will relate to one another in a way that no one else can or will experience from either one of us. We will love and care for each other particularly and specially.

Three times in chapter 4 and again in chapter 5 of the Song of Songs, the husband refers to his wife as "my sister, my bride." Calling his wife "my sister" of course sounds concerning to us today, but at the time of writing and during Jesus' time, the sibling relationship was considered the strongest relationship one could have.[3]

The heart is the place of deepest desires and motivations. "Set me as a seal upon your heart, as a seal upon your arm," the beloved says (Song 8:6). By the first century, this verse would be seen as a way for the husband to say, "You are my closest companion, my best friend, my strongest bond." In turn, the wife states it's there that "I am going to seal you as my husband." They both promise that *in everything I say or do, I will be committed to you.*

COVENANTAL COMMITMENT

Marriage isn't a side gig or weekend hobby. You say things to your spouse and only your spouse, and do things with your spouse and only your spouse, that speak to a whole life commitment between you. In marriage, you are every day saying, "I am going to be with you, and I'm so much going to be with you that it is going to be almost impossible to break the seal between us."

To talk about belonging to one another, of being exclusively committed to one another, is to talk about covenant. The word "covenant" is the biblical word often used to describe the marriage relationship.[4] Covenant speaks to how the husband and wife have a unique, committed relationship to one another. They are obligated to one another, bound to one another in ways specific to their relationship. They are promising to be in an exclusive relationship with each other.

Notably, God's relationship with His people is described in terms of a covenant. Discussion on this covenant has often compared it to other ancient treaties of that time period, and the covenant between God and Israel is indeed set up like an ancient treaty. However, it does not stop there. Marriage, too, is covenantal. It is "a sacred bond that is characterized by permanence, sacredness, intimacy, mutuality and exclusiveness." From what is said, we see that the husband "gave [a] solemn oath (pledged faith) to the wife and entered into a covenant not intended to be broken."[5]

This is what God does with Israel. God publicly marries His people at Sinai. As He continues to relate to them, He regularly reminds them that their relationship is a covenant held together by promise and the obligation to be committed to each other. God says as much to Israel in Ezekiel 16:8: "I made my vow to you and entered into a covenant with you, declares the Lord God, and you became mine." The metaphor is referring to "a common practice of public covenanting, involving the exchange of vows, as part of entering into marriage."[6]

And so God commits Himself to Israel out of all the nations in the earth. The union is sealed in a covenantal ceremony—as a marriage ceremony—whereby God and His people would be exclusively committed to each other. God and His people belong to one another and as such are obligated to one another in ways specific to their relationship.

The Ten Commandments are, in a sense, marital vows. The very first commandment is all about commitment. Israel was to only worship the Lord as God, and He alone would be their husband. The rest of the commandments then lay out the specific ways this commitment will play out in their life together.

So when God's people follow after other gods, their actions are framed, not surprisingly, as a betrayal of their commitment to God.

Commitment in marriage means you don't fool around with other people. You don't engage with them in ways that should be exclusive to your spouse. For Israel, this meant not taking after the customs of the surrounding nations and in particular not worshiping their gods.

> **Only the language of adultery captures the reality of the commitment Israel was to have to God, and what a big deal it was when they badly betrayed that commitment.**

This idolatry was disloyalty to God and is explicitly described as being like adultery. It is the steepest violation you can make to a committed relationship. It's adultery because God's people were to be exclusively committed to Him. Only the language of adultery captures the reality of the commitment Israel was to have to God, and what a big deal it was when they badly betrayed that commitment. Israel didn't just have friendly chats with other gods; they whored after other gods (Judg. 2:17; Ezek. 16), and in so doing betrayed their commitment to the Lord, who has all along been a faithful and committed husband to His people. They betrayed God in how they sought the help and protection of others besides Him (e.g., Egypt, Assyria).

This is a common theme in the Old Testament prophets— Israel as the cheating wife of God, the loving, faithful husband.[7] God recalls the previous devoted commitment of Israel as a bride (Jer. 2:2), who has now become a serial adulterer: "You have played the whore with many lovers" (Jer. 3:1). "Surely, as a treacherous wife leaves her husband, so have you been treacherous to me, O house of Israel, declares the LORD" (3:20).

Sadly, this characterizes most of the history of God and His people in the Bible. Israel on multiple occasions "cheats" on God, breaks the exclusive commitment they should have had with the Lord, and pursues other lovers (Hos. 2:5) by their worship of idols.

HOSEA AND GOMER

A legitimate question arises at this point: Does God even want to stay in this marriage, given the propensity of His people to regularly cheat on Him? He certainly has the right to leave, since His people have not kept up their side of the covenant commitment.

The answer as to the nature of God's commitment is seen in the life of Hosea. This story cements how we can understand God's commitment to His faithless people. You might remember that by God's directive—"Go and take"—Hosea the prophet marries Gomer. But Gomer cheats on him and runs away to live a grossly immoral life. She gets sold into slavery. This is her just deserts, given her actions.

Hosea would have been justified in putting her aside. But instead, God directs Hosea to find her, buy her out of slavery— i.e., redeem her—to love her, to bring her back home. The book of Hosea shows a God who recommits to His people—not in an obligatory way but with a willing, steadfast love. God's illustration using Hosea and Gomer is a foreshadowing of what He does through Jesus.

As Matthew Haste notes, "In Hosea 3, the prophet himself redeems his wife, this time receiving the command, 'Go yet, love a woman' . . . instead of the less romantic 'Go and take' of 1:2."[8] Derek Kidner's summary articulates the significance of this passage for the present subject: "It is all of grace, and it clothes the new covenant in wedding garb. It makes three things very plain:

the permanence of this union, the intimacy of it, and the fact that it owes everything to God."[9]

In having Hosea marry an immoral woman (possibly a prostitute at the time of the marriage) and then go seek her out even after her adultery, God shows us something about how He relates to His people. Here we see that God's commitment is such that even when we fail in our part of the commitment, God won't fail. God is always ready and willing to find us and bring us back into relationship with Him. His commitment is strong enough for both sides of the relationship.

> "I will betroth you to me forever. . . . I will betroth you to me in faithfulness. And you shall know the LORD."

In Hosea 2:15–23, God declares how He will bring it about so that Israel no longer seeks after Baal but will once again call the Lord "my Husband." He will make this happen by removing "the names of the Baals from her mouth." Then the Lord makes as strong of a commitment to Israel as could be made. In some of the most beautiful and binding words in all of Scripture, He says to her, "And I will betroth you to me forever. I will betroth you to me in righteousness and in justice, in steadfast love and in mercy. I will betroth you to me in faithfulness. And you shall know the LORD."

By all reasonable measures, the Lord should give up on Israel. Yet He won't do it; His heart is still for Israel. Hear God's longing, His emotion:

> How can I give you up, O Ephraim? How can I hand
> you over, O Israel? How can I make you like Admah?
> How can I treat you like Zeboiim? My heart recoils
> within me; my compassion grows warm and tender.

I will not execute my burning anger; I will not again destroy Ephraim; for I am God and not a man, the Holy One in your midst, and I will not come in wrath. (Hos. 11:8–9)

The prophet Hosea's marriage to Gomer is itself meant to be a living picture of God's marriage to Israel, and specifically His willingness to still commit to Israel even though Israel has been faithless. "And the LORD said to me, 'Go again, love a woman who is loved by another man and is an adulteress, even as the LORD loves the children of Israel, though they turn to other gods and love cakes of raisins'" (3:1).

God is willing to "remarry" His people. His commitment to them pushes through even their lack of commitment to Him. The repetition in 2:19–20, "I will betroth you . . . I will betroth you to me . . . I will betroth you to me" emphasizes God's commitment to Israel. The past will be put away, they will start over, and this time it will stick.[10]

GOD'S UNFAILING *HESED*

Hosea is not the only biblical book that reiterates this message. In Ezekiel 16:59–60, after a lengthy and explicit recitation of Israel's adulterous idolatry and the consequences that will come because of their actions, God still commits to a relationship with Israel.

For thus says the Lord GOD: I will deal with you as you have done, you who have despised the oath in breaking the covenant, yet I will remember my covenant with you in the days of your youth, and I will establish for you an everlasting covenant.

This is why the Hebrew word *hesed* is used in reference to God. This word is usually translated as "steadfast love." God has *hesed* for His people—He has a loyal, committed love for them. His love remains even when the relationship is betrayed. For even when Israel's sinful adultery has all but destroyed their relationship with God, God's *hesed* means there is commitment from God, and thus an always ready grace to restore and repair the broken relationship. God's love for His beloved people is a committed love, bringing both undeserved deliverance and promised divine faithfulness to them.[11]

The Lord persistently says to Israel, "I have loved you with an everlasting love; therefore I have continued my faithfulness to you" (Jer. 31:3).

What God does with Israel is a foreshadowing of what we see later in the New Testament. What was true for Israel becomes even more evident as marriage between God and Israel becomes the marriage between Jesus and the church. Jesus is the definitive answer to how God can have and stay in a committed relationship with His people.

JESUS: GOD'S ULTIMATE COMMITMENT

With Jesus we have the strongest expression possible of the Lord's commitment to us. It is represented in the very nature of Jesus, that the second person of the Trinity takes on humanity. In Jesus Himself—fully God and fully man—is the union of God and humanity. And Jesus retains this even now—this fully God and fully man nature—and will retain this into eternity.

Nothing says commitment more than the eternal God being willing in some mysterious but legitimate and wondrous way to bring into Himself, into His very being, the human nature of His people.

But it's even more than that, as demonstrated in how Jesus willingly gives up His life for our sake, taking on Himself the consequences of our sinful betrayal of God. Yes, the Lord God was so committed to us He was willing to die for us in order to restore relationship with us—yes, even our fickle, serial-cheating, two-timing, idolatrous selves.

This is why Jesus Himself then is the means by which we can be the committed and faithful bride of our Lord. For Jesus not only takes away our unfaithful spirit, He gives us His own spirit, one that can be committed and faithful to God. This is why Jesus can say to His disciples that He will be with them always (Matt. 28:20). And later we have the promise in Hebrews 13:5 that the Lord "will never leave you nor forsake you."

Jesus Himself enables the promise of Jeremiah 31:31–34 to come to fruition: that the bond, the commitment, between us and God can form and not ever be broken. Because now the commitment exists within our own hearts, because Jesus is Himself in our hearts. Once Jesus comes in by way of the Spirit, He remakes us in our very inner being so that we have the virtues of love and grace and righteousness that can translate to faithful commitment to the Lord.

Commitment to the Lord leads to and is the basis for commitment to one another. Our vows to the Lord as His people, married to Him, are lived out through our acting in commitment to one another.

Having Jesus in us enables us to be committed to the Lord. So Paul reminds us in Galatians 3:20 that we live the life of Christ, since Christ now lives in us because of Christ's committed love for us. Or in 2 Corinthians 11:2–3, Paul shows his concern that the Corinthian church realize that their relationship with the Lord is one of "sincere and pure devotion." This is not a superficial occasional partnership. It is a committed relationship.

Commitment to the Lord leads to and is the basis for commitment to one another. Our vows to the Lord as His people, married to Him, are lived out through our acting in commitment to one another.

If we are faithful to the Lord, we must be faithful to the Lord's beloved, the church. The strength of our bond to God, established in Christ, is the strength we depend on in our bond to one another in the church. If we are faithful to the Lord by virtue of God's power working within us by faith in Jesus, we will be faithful to one another by that same power.

THE CHURCH: NOT JUST ANOTHER GROUP

We can't ignore, however, the increasing ways people are isolated and separated from one another today. We have fewer long-lasting relationships in our lives. Robert Putnam's book *Bowling Alone* notes, for example, the decline in membership of civic associations.[12] There has been a steep decline in active involvement that requires face-to-face, in-person interaction and relationship. Fewer people are making the commitment to be part of rotary clubs, PTAs, bowling leagues, or churches.

Some of the reasons for this are increased busyness and the added stresses that brings. Other reasons are tied to general apathy matched with the attraction of settling for television or browsing the internet from the comfort of home.

When it comes to the church, we find multiple reasons why people are less willing to commit to one another. Some have experienced hurts from betrayals within past church relationships, creating lingering mistrust. Many reasons why people are leery of committing to a community of believers are very serious—issues we should be empathetic about. These would include things like abuse of power. Neglect of shepherding care. Unbiblical teaching or immoral behavior within leadership. Even friendships that turn out to be superficial leave a stain.

Yet there is much lost when we are not willing to find a church family in which we'll commit to one another. We are not meant to endlessly wander, to be unattached to anyone or anything. We are meant for relationship, for community. And we only get the most of our relationships and community when we are committed to one another over an extended time. There are ways I am known and know others in my own community over the last twenty years that at this point can never be replicated. They can love me and I can love them with twenty years of committed relationship informing and backing up our every interaction.

The key to having relationships like this comes as we remember that our relationship with Jesus is the one committed relationship that has never failed. And it is on the basis of that divine relationship that we can enter into committed relationships with one another. What we depend on then in our relationships is not our strength to stay committed to other believers. What we depend on is God's strength in us.

Every time we think of our committed relationship with God to us, we are reminded of the God who is behind that commitment. God's love is stronger than death (Song 8:6). His commitment to us is based on love for us as His bride, and it is stronger than the most powerful killer in the universe.

It is this stronger-than-death love that is in us and runs through us to one another in close bonds. It is a divine fire that can't be quenched or drowned.

And it is this love, this *hesed* love—loyal, steadfast, committed love—this divine fire kind of love—that has been extended to us and given to us to, in turn, extend to one another.

That enables us to go from being casual and superficial with one another to being beloved and committed to each other. We have a love within us and between us that is stronger than death. It is stronger than past hurts, stronger than current controversies and tensions, stronger than miscommunication or personal failures or awkward personalities.

> When we talk about church membership, what we are doing is inviting people into a relationship of committed love to one another. We make a mistake if church membership is spoken of or lived out as something similar to joining a company or a club.

Church membership is one of the practical ways we can publicly acknowledge, affirm, and reinforce our commitment to one another in the Lord. When we talk about church membership, what we are doing is inviting people into a relationship of committed love to one another. We make a mistake if church membership is spoken of or lived out as something similar to joining a company or a club. Relationships that are based in the love of God give us incentive toward mutual encouragement and care. They also give our relationships the motivation to not ignore when there are differences or breakdowns in our relationships; instead, because of our love for one another, we will address sin and engage in practices of confession, repentance, and repair so we can remain in committed love with one another. It also provides the boundaries of mutual belief and faith we need to make sure we are committed to move together in the same direction.

One important way we can verbally reinforce and affirm commitment to one another is through reciting church creeds together. Creeds said together are a way in which everyone is saying, "This is what I believe and I believe it together with you and I want to continue to believe it together with you."[13] Some churches use a responsive reading, a statement of faith, a communal reading of Scripture, or a benediction to join voices affirming their fellowship in Christ.

Often the songs in a worship service voice the beliefs of the faith, and there is power in singing together with others in the congregation.

What binds us together is not having the same opinions or liking the same hobbies, but instead what binds us together is the love of God.

But also within the church, we find many noticeable and other not so noticeable but still significant ways for us to express and affirm commitment to one another.

It's when people don't rush out after a church gathering but intentionally stay longer, delaying lunch or afternoon TV in order to greet someone new or pray for someone who is struggling.

It's when people commit to working out a tension between them over a planned lunch or coffee together, or by inviting others in the community to help them resolve their tension. It's when they don't give up after one meeting together but continue to stay in prayer and conversation with one another.

It's when people meet together regularly in small groups or Bible studies or Sunday school classes, building and growing relationships with one another over many years.

Some of the people you are in relationship with are a hot mess. Some have habits and preferences very different from yours. Some have thoughts on culture and politics that frustrate you. But in Christ, we can still be committed to one another, as long as what binds us together is not having the same opinions or liking the same hobbies, but instead, what binds us together is the love of God. This is a love-fueled commitment that is stronger than death, stronger than past hurts, stronger than present controversies.

God has committed Himself to us forever. And so we are committed to one another forever.

Chapter 9

PASSION

I've enjoyed watching professional football since I was in grade school.

I like turning on the television during football season and watching whatever NFL games are on. But my feelings about football go to another level when it comes to my favorite team, the New York Jets (*Go Jets!*). I don't just watch the Jets; I am deeply, wholly invested in cheering for the Jets. I jump up and run around the room when they are doing well in a game. I collapse on the floor in disbelief and emotional pain when they are doing badly. As I hinted in chapter 1, when it comes to the Jets, I don't just like them, I am passionate about them!

GOD'S PASSION

The word "passion" describes having an intense feeling over something. Passion is when you have outsized emotion toward something compared to other things. Someone may like a sport, but they are passionate about their local team—passionately rooting for the home team, passionately opposing their rivals. Someone may enjoy the great outdoors, but they are especially passionate when they not only get to be outside but go on a hike or camping trip. Another likes hearing birds sing, but someone else might be passionate about identifying species, and won't go out without binoculars. Many people like to cook, but some people are passionate about it, experimenting with herbs and spices and ethnic flavors, honing a recipe until it's just right.

Those are examples of passion in relation to an activity or hobby. Passion is also a dynamic in relationships. Passion in a relationship speaks to having a strong and particular pull toward another person. You experience a sweet joy when things are good with someone else, real sorrow when things are difficult, great distress and even anger when you are in conflict. You have these outsized emotions because of how invested you are in the other person. This is not someone you're indifferent to or even someone you merely like; but someone you deeply care about, with whom you have a relationship that matters and you would not let go of or want to see end. You will do all that you can to maintain the relationship.

God has outsized emotion for His people. He passionately loves us. He has put His affection on us and deeply cares about and is invested in being in relationship with us. The Lord says in Deuteronomy 7:7 that He has "set his love" on His people. As Daniel Block observes, the term translated "set his love" in Deuteronomy is meant "to express YHWH's passion for his people and his people's passion toward him."[1]

The Lord has everything; all things belong to Him. Yet He displays passion for us: "Behold, to the LORD your God belong heaven and the heaven of heavens, the earth with all that is in it. Yet the LORD set his heart in love on your fathers and chose their offspring after them, you above all peoples, as you are this day" (Deut. 10:14–15). The same Hebrew word, translated "set his love" in Deuteronomy 7:7, is used here in the phrase "set his heart." This term describes a passionate "pursuit of [a] partner."[2]

Perhaps you've received news of someone who made a foolish, even dangerous decision. Likely your reaction was more passionate if the person is someone you're close to than if what you heard about involved a mere acquaintance. We see this with God. In Isaiah 54:6–8, we see the Lord's passion expressesd in "overflowing anger" over Israel's sinful betrayal of their relationship. But it's also shown in His "great compassion" and "everlasting love" to call her back to Himself because He is passionate about His relationship with Israel. Not only that, but He declares His intention to rejoice over Israel, to "exult over [Israel] with loud singing" (Zeph. 3:17). He doesn't just hum a few bars. His passionate love for Israel is so strong it "cannot be contained but bursts into elated singing."[3] What we see here is a love from God that is "wholehearted, enthusiastic, not grudging, not holding back at all."[4]

GOD'S JEALOUSY

As we discussed in chapter 1, words of love expressed between a husband and wife in the Song of Songs echoes how the Lord relates to us. The Lord is passionate about His beloved people. You and I are especially desired by God. More than the stars. More than the oceans. More than the angels themselves. We are desired by the Lord, passionately so. God looks at us and says, "Yes, I really want you—and I want you to desire Me above all others!"

The biblical description that well captures God's passion for us is that God is a "jealous" God. That is to say, His passion and fervor are for an exclusive, committed relationship with His people.[5] He had bluntly warned the nation of Israel against worshiping any but Himself: "You shall worship no other god, for the LORD, whose name is Jealous, is a jealous God" (Ex. 34:14). His jealousy isn't a petty feeling of envy, but a jealousy that guards the exclusivity and faithfulness of a relationship; remember that God looks at His people, His beloved, as His bride.

He describes the consequences of betrayal to the covenant:

> "You shall not bow down to [idols] or serve them, for I the Lord your God am a jealous God, visiting the iniquity of the fathers on the children to the third and the fourth generation of those who hate me." (Ex. 20:5)

Here the passion of God for His people shows in His righteous judgment on His people if they betray their commitment to God and go after idols.

God's jealousy is tied to the covenant—the committed relationship Israel has with God. He expects His people to be passionately committed to Him just as He is passionately committed to them. He is zealous to protect His exclusive relationship with Israel and will passionately stand against anything that might compromise His relationship with Israel.

GOD'S PURSUIT

All these passages describe the intensity of God's desire for us, His ardor for an exclusive relationship with us. The descriptions of the jealousy of God leading to wrathful judgment are not God suddenly flying off the handle and losing His temper. The Lord's anger when it comes to His people is not arbitrary or random. His jealousy for us comes out of the fervent passion He has for us. To break faith with God by following other gods will indeed "provoke him to anger" (Deut. 4:25; 32:16) because it is the most severe kind of betrayal to the relationship: the spiritual equivalent of sleeping around on the spouse you promised to be faithful to for life.

The Lord's anger is the anger of a spurned spouse who is passionately committed to the relationship. Tim Keller called it "love fighting extinction," adding that "godly jealousy is angered love that stays love and stays committed to rescuing that crumbling love relationship and getting that person back."[6] Ray Ortlund describes it as an "aching longing for their restoration."[7]

The passion of God for us means He will never "check out" of the relationship.

God is not looking for a casual relationship with us, but a deeply intimate committed relationship. As such, the passion of God for us means He will never check out of the relationship. He will never be all right with a relationship where we live under the same roof but live separate lives. God's passion for us is to have a relationship where the default state is steadfast, abiding, intimate love. God is always seeking after us, always investing the very best of Himself into His relationship with us.

Many of us have learned to recite Psalm 23, and we're encouraged that His "goodness and mercy shall follow me" (v. 6). The Hebrew word translated "follow" here is *radap*. But it's stronger than our English word. David Lamb writes,

> The Hebrew verb *radap* is usually translated in verse 6 as "follow." . . . But as we look at how this verb is used elsewhere, we discover it has a much more active sense. It usually appears in military contexts. Pharaoh pursued (*radap)* Israel at the Red Sea (Ex. 14:4). Israel pursued (*radap*) the Philistines after David defeated Goliath (1 Sam. 17:52). Saul frequently pursued (*radap*) David to kill him. . . . "Follow" is too passive for *radap*. God's

goodness and his *hesed*-love won't just follow after us, they will pursue and chase us, stalk and hunt us.[8]

Those are strong words: God will chase and hunt us down if that's what it takes to rescue us. He fiercely pursues us and fights for the relationship, zealous to care for and protect His people. All of this is an expression of His unique and specific love for His people. "If the Lord burns with jealousy for His people, He is set on protecting them and His holy character of love."[9]

His passion for us, to pursue us, even when we wander away from Him or break our marital commitment to Him, is most shown in His willingness to suffer and die for us in order to forever secure our relationship with Him. To say that Jesus loves the church to the point of giving up His life for her shows how strongly He feels about His people. We can rightly describe this love as a love "strong as death, jealousy . . . fierce as the grave" (Song 8:6).

This is a love full of fervor and passion. It burns as hot as a fire, not to destroy others but instead to warm, excite, and comfort others. It is love that cannot be quenched or drowned (v.7), but always vigorously yearns for the beloved. This love is divine love, for it is "the very flame of the Lord."

Here again, the mention of it being a "jealous" love speaks to strong, focused passion for the beloved. To say it is "as strong as death" points to its powerful, intentional intensity. Divine love is like death in that there is no letup in death's pursuit of human beings. So also there is no letup in divine love. Death will eventually claim every human life. So also divine love will always eventually find and claim its beloved for itself.

The Lord's love for us never loses its intensity or fervor.

This is why passionate love at its best and purest is divine love. It is a love of unrelenting, vigorous pursuit.

This speaks to the unique fervor of God's love. Human beings can fall passionately in love. But the passionate fervor of that love can waver or falter over time. The heat of the relationship in the early months or years of the relationship can lessen and become less like a raging fire and more like a slowly fading campfire.

The Lord's love for us, however, never loses its intensity or fervor. To say that "many waters cannot quench love, neither can floods drown it" (Song 8:7) is to speak of love that burns even in the face of trying circumstances and relational letdowns—that burns even through our disobedient betrayal. Even the prospect of death on the cross did not slow down the Lord's pursuit of us, or His loving embrace of us now that He has us.

GOD'S ENDURANCE

The climax of the opening ceremonies of the Olympics is the lighting of the cauldron. This cauldron is lit from a torch that is said, in the lore surrounding the games (if not literally so), to have remained lit since the first Olympics. It symbolizes the enduring nature of life, hope, and the competitive spirit.

In the same way, divine love is a love that endures, that always burns with the same strength and intensity for us. It burns for us, always burns for us, will never stop burning for us.

When you look at another believer, you are seeing someone who is intensely, ardently loved by God. So when we consider how to relate

By virtue of our faith in God and the indwelling of the Spirit of God, we now readily have within us the kind of love that will persist in its passion for others.

to such a person God cares about so much, all the more it means we should care about them with the same ardor and passion.

To care about someone only casually or superficially whom our Lord cares about so passionately goes against the Spirit of God within us. By His Spirit, we love others in the church with ardor and fervent desire. We don't just put up with each other but show passionate love for one another. To demonstrate such love, as flawed humans struggling with a sin nature, we must tap into His divine love, "the very flame of the Lord." Does this sound too hard? What about that person with the annoying habits? The one who's always late? That person who is critical or unappreciative? The person who has poor social cues? Here's our answer: by virtue of our faith in God and the indwelling of the Spirit of God, we now readily have within us the kind of love that can persist in its passion for others.

Passionate love will have the following implications:

Passionate love means deliberate relationship

Love that is passionate is a love that prioritizes relationship with others. This means effort is made to regularly spend time with people. It means intentional, deliberate, and regular investments of care and affection into relationships. Beloved love necessitates routine interactions with the same people in the same spaces.[10]

I did a funeral recently for one of the longtime members of my church. At the funeral I learned that another member of my church had been friends with this recently passed member for a number of years. I was surprised, as there was a significant age gap between these individuals. In addition, they were of different ethnic backgrounds, and held different social inclinations and political preferences.

Yet they had a legitimate and strong relationship with each other. The younger person often would visit the older one, spending time with her and helping with various errands. Their relationship with one another was intentional and deliberate. They had to make time for each other for it to work. And they did. Because they had love for one another in Christ, they regularly and consistently developed a relationship of care and affection.

The best relationships do not happen by accident. They happen from seeing people around, and then intentionally pursuing relationship with them. And this is not a one and done task. We must be passionate about continuing to deliberately be in relationship, to spend the time and have the consistency such that the relationship might continue and grow. For any relationship—even the best ones—are more fragile than you might imagine. They are like a plant you may have in your home. It looks healthy and beautiful. But that's only if you take care of it. It will die within a few weeks if you don't water it, if you keep it out of the sun, if you completely ignore it. So also our relationships require deliberate effort to start and deliberate effort to keep them going. Passionate love means regularly putting the water and sun of time and care into our relationships.

Passionate love means a persistent pursuit of the other

Beloved love notices when others are drifting out of their relationships and their community, or when someone goes missing from the fellowship of the body. It means we more intently pursue relationships with those new to our community. We especially more intensely pursue relationships with those who are most overlooked, most on the edges of community.

A number of years ago, "M" joined our church. M has struggled with homelessness for most of her life, and has various mental, physical, and social challenges. Her lack of social graces, such as her tendency to interrupt conversations or ask random questions at the wrong time, makes her the kind of person "ordinary" people aren't naturally enthusiastic about getting to know. It's why I've been so encouraged by the people in our community who have formed a relationship with her. In particular, one of our deacons who also happens to be one of the best Bible teachers in our city intentionally established a relationship with her. When M asked if she and another similarly challenged friend of hers could find someone to teach them the Bible, this deacon, who already has a full schedule, immediately set up a regular meeting with M and her friend. She has joyfully attached herself to M and pursued relationship with her. This is what divine love expressed in passionate pursuit of others should look like.

Passionate love means acting to restore broken relationships because of how passionately we care about being in relationship with one another

On a few occasions, I've had some conflict with a leader at our church. In one particular case, the leader had been critical about me in ways that upset me, and I reacted defensively, though in truth, I could understand where he was coming from. What I eventually felt I needed to do (with the encouragement of others to help me with my initial reluctance) was talk with him and work things out as much as we could. So I did meet with him and talk with him. It took multiple meetings and multiple conversations. And the motivating factor here was that both he and I cared about the relationship, one built over the course of a decade, and so we wanted to make an effort to maintain the relationship, even with our differences.

The end of this story isn't that we found total agreement on everything. What we did find though, was that God's passionate love within us—because it is stronger than death—is more powerful than past hurts or controversies or differences. That has proven to be the case for every community and every relationship I've had that has also depended on this same love.

Passionate love means caring about the holiness and purity of the church

The Lord passionately cares about His people being spiritually whole and beautiful. He loves us with the goal of our being "holy and without blemish" (Eph. 5:27). We exhibit this same care when we are willing to address sin within our community. This is commonly referred to as church discipline.

Church discipline, done rightly, is an act of passionate love for one another. It means we care enough about our relationships to say something or do something when we see others wallowing in sinful messiness. It's not loving if we ignore it when people we are in relationship with are falling away from God. It's not loving if we are passive when people we are in a relationship with act in abusive or harmful ways to those around them. Passionate love speaks up and speaks into people's lives. Passionate love continues to pursue people even when it is uncomfortable, even when they reject our words and dismiss our actions. Passionate love means we bear even all of that, for it is a love that can bear all things and endure all things, for the sake of a community that is more beautifully holy before the Lord. The process of church discipline is really a prayerful process of love of others for the hope of a beautiful restoration of people drawing back to God, back into His love and our love.

What we must try and see is what the Lord sees that His people can be and will be one day—the holy and pure bride of Christ, radiant in her splendor and beauty. The more clearly we can see what the Lord sees when He looks at us, the more it will energize us to love others around us, and to do so with the kind of fervency and drive that comes the more you know what is to come.

Chapter 10

CONFLICT

During my senior year of college, my friend Joe and I would often play video games in the afternoon before heading out for track practice.

We played games that involved us competing against one another. We were in general very competitive with each other, no matter what we were doing. And so that included whatever video games we were playing. We actually had a no-mercy rule, which meant that even if you were winning by a lot you could still run up the score on the other person. That rule, along with more than a little bit of trash talking, meant that, not surprisingly, we sometimes got a little heated.

One time, we were playing Madden NFL, and I was up by four touchdowns. As I started increasing my lead, going for extra points in keeping with the no-mercy rule, Joe, who had already muttered more than a few angry words in my direction, finally exploded. He accused me of winning only by luck and not having any skill. He knew me well enough to know that this would press my buttons. I stood up, then Joe stood up; soon we were in each other's faces, yelling at each other.

We soon backed down, and by the next day we had gotten over it and reconciled. Looking back on this moment, I remember clearly just how mad I was, and how especially mad I was because it was a conflict with someone I was close with. In fact, his words and his actions made me angrier than I ever would have been if I was playing a game with a random person. It was the close relationship that made the conflict especially explosive.

Our friendship continued after that conflict. But many relationships slowly disintegrate and fall apart because of conflict, which has the power to break relationships apart. It can break apart even our closest relationships, like marriage.

STUCK IN CONFLICT

Sometimes it's one key but major incident that causes the break. Other times it is an accumulation of infractions, misunderstandings, or unresolved tensions that crack the relationship until it breaks. But when the break happens, what then settles into the middle of the relationship is conflict. And conflict, depending on what it is, and how long it lasts, can become the final word on the relationship. Everything that was good and memorable gets absorbed into the difficulty, ending in the black hole of conflict. The friendship, the partnership, the marriage—conflict makes them into a past friendship, a former partnership, an ex-marriage, and those relationships from that point on will be defined and bound by the conflict that made them past, former, ex.

My wife and I have had some significant arguments in our marriage. Some of these have lasted for several hours. When there is an unresolved issue, it sits there between us, affecting every interaction, every casual glance. We still have to do the ordinary things that keep our house running—get the kids up and to school, prep for and eat meals, clean up. All those things are done, yet under the foreboding eyes of the conflict. Our relationship can't be anything more than these perfunctory things as long as the conflict remains between us. For as long as it lasts, it defines the relationship; indeed, it is the relationship.

Conflicts are especially potent in a marriage relationship in terms of their destructive power. This is because marriage involves intimate union with another person. When conflict arises here, it immediately strikes at the most vulnerable parts of ourselves. It touches on the broadest range of ourselves. Thus the conflict quickly takes on heightened significance and influence. It always has the potential to be more serious, and thus potentially more damaging, given that the battle is happening in such dangerous territory. The same tools that help nurture a marriage— our words, our shared experiences—turn into the kindling of harsh words and criticism or grudges over past events. And all this makes the conflict burn hot and remain hot and, left undealt with, can be fatally destructive to the relationship.

Conflicts come in all shapes and sizes. But the following are three broad types of conflict in a marriage relationship.

Hostility

This is a "hot" kind of conflict. You are outright opposed to the other person. Any number of things can incite this. It could be something serious, like a betrayal. It could be something somewhat incidental, like a poorly planned outing, keys being misplaced yet again, disagreement over what the plans actually were for the weekend. But it sparks something deeper that leads to direct hostile conflict. You become actively angry at your spouse.

Disconnection

This is a slow burn kind of conflict. You are in a relationship where you feel alone and isolated. This often happens because of life circumstances such as a sudden illness, financial hardship, busy schedules. It all leads to isolation and disconnection, where your spouse becomes a stranger to you and someone you find yourself pulling away from rather than being drawn to. This can be the hardest kind of conflict to unravel, as there is not one specific thing to address but the slow buildup of a lot of things.

Rejection

This might not be outward hostility, but the impact of rejection is very similar to outward hostility. You may still share the same house and are still in contact, but it's clear that you no longer want or desire each other. You have rejected each another as a spouse. There's no attempt to address the issues between you, to seek understanding and forgiveness. Instead, you each feel apathy when it comes to how the other person thinks or feels. They are more like a roommate or co-parent to you as opposed to a spouse.

CONFLICT WITH GOD

We've talked about how the Bible describes God as being married to His people. We aren't telling the full story, however, if we don't consider to what extent conflict has defined that relationship. The conflict in this relationship has gone through all three versions of conflict we just listed: hostility, disconnection, rejection. This progression is clearly exemplified in the book of Hosea with a startling illustration as we read about in chapter 8 on commitment.

God has instructed his prophet Hosea to "take to yourself a wife of whoredom . . ." (Hos. 1:2). In obedience, he married Gomer. We might wonder why God would command such a thing, but we understand when we read the strong language in the rest of verse 2: "For the land commits great whoredom by forsaking the LORD."

Clearly, there is hostility between God and Israel. Israel has cheated on Him by following after idols. Gomer, the "wife of whoredom," is an apt picture of Israel's unfaithfulness—such a betrayal brings outright conflict between God and Israel. God tells His people they will "reap the whirlwind" of His righteous outrage over their sinful betrayal (Hos. 8:7). Indeed, because of the adultery of the nation, God is opposed to them and is now fighting against her (Hos. 2:11; 5:12, 14; 13:7–9).

Here is disconnection and finally rejection. God even says He will drive Israel "out of my house. I will love them no more" (9:15). Remembering the importance of presence as we covered in chapter 7, we see how serious these words are. Israel has brought Him to the very point of no longer even wanting her around. Because the people will no longer listen to Him, "God will reject them" (9:17).

The case is made clear in Hosea that the people are in conflict with God and disconnected from Him, which would fully justify His being done with them. But that's not what happens. By the end of Hosea, God promises to "heal their apostasy," to turn His anger away from them and once again "love them freely" (14:14).

So why didn't God go all the way through with it and permanently dispense Himself of Israel? It's because of how dominant grace is within the personhood of God. God is fully just and, thankfully, He is also fully gracious.

His love travels down the road of grace to find and reconcile with His bride.

What God does in the book of Hosea is a placeholder for what Jesus ultimately does, and we see this dramatically illustrated in the way Hosea sought after Gomer. Jesus is God showing that He still intends to see this marriage to His people work. This does not mean God ignores the conflict. Instead, God heads right into the heart of it. He does this as a function of His love for us and grace toward us.

His love travels down the road of grace to find and reconcile with His bride. Indeed, the most important ingredient to holding on to love through conflict is grace.

GOD'S GRACE TRUMPS CONFLICT

Yes, conflict brings division and separation. But the grace of God always wins out to cross the divide and bring healing and reconciliation in any conflict. In Isaiah 54:7–8, the Lord talks about how His anger caused a rift between Him and His people. But it was only for "a brief moment," for as righteous as God's anger is, He always also has compassion and everlasting love to cover over that anger so that rather than stay separated from His people, He moves toward them to gather them to Himself.

All of this is grace. That God would instead be willing to show love and compassion rather than anger, that He would seek reconciliation with us rather than continued division and separation.

John Calvin notes that even with our sin, God "still finds something to love. However much we may be sinners by our fault, we nevertheless remain his creatures. However much we have brought death upon ourselves, yet he has created us unto life. Thus he is moved by pure and freely given love of us to receive us into grace."[1]

> Always pay attention to places in the Bible where God describes Himself. God in those places is saying, "Here is how I want you to think about Me. Here is especially what should come to mind."

Grace is what kept God in relationship with us despite the conflict. Love is what motivated God in Jesus to move through the conflict to find us on the other side of the breach and then lead us back to unity with him.

What we see from God then is the willingness to not give up, to instead pursue us and work out the conflict between us. This is all a function of the grace of God. To understand how we can be in relationship even with conflict, we must look to the grace of God. Grace is a fundamental and primary characteristic of God. Grace exists because God exists. Here is what Moses experienced:

> The LORD descended in the cloud and stood with him there, and proclaimed the name of the LORD. The LORD passed before him and proclaimed, "The LORD, the LORD, a God merciful and gracious, slow to anger, and abounding in steadfast love and faithfulness." (Ex. 34:5–6)

Always pay attention to places in the Bible where God describes Himself. God in those places is saying, "Here is how I want you to think about Me. Here is especially what should come to mind."

Knowing God means knowing that He is a God of grace. He is a God who shows favor toward us. He could show complete fairness, which would mean holding us immediately accountable and judging us for being a people who disobey and rebel against Him. Do the crime, do the time.

But that's not what God does. He delays judgment; He holds it back. He is patient with us, showing goodness and love toward us, which is summed up most especially in sending Jesus so that we might find life and salvation by faith in Christ.

In fact, the major accent of God's relationship toward us is grace. We don't have a God who is simply gracious, but one who is abundant in grace. Imagine that we instead had a God who was abundant in swift wrath and stingy and slow in giving grace;

if God was like this, we would not be able to use the terms we instead use when describing God.

Because God is not only gracious but abundant in grace, we can talk about having a relationship of love, of being beloved to God. It's because God allows His grace to essentially veto His right to bring immediate justice on us and instead show His goodness toward us by creating space and opportunity for us to be restored to close relationship with Him, to remain "married" to Him.

> **Because of God's grace we can remain in close relationship with Him even in conflict. This same grace is how we can figure out a way to also remain in close relationship with each other when we have conflict.**

It is God's grace that characterizes Him to not distance Himself from us over conflict, but instead keeps in relationship with us and reaches out to us with undeserved yet freely and generously given favor and kindness.

Our whole relationship with God is based on grace! Ephesians 2:8–9 reminds us, "For by grace you have been saved through faith, and this is not your own doing; it is the gift of God."

Our salvation and subsequent relationship with God comes from grace. Grace is completely alien to the human heart. Nothing about us can or is able to generate the kind of grace we need for a life with God. And so that's why God brings the grace we need; in fact, He generously gives us the "riches of his grace," whereby our sinful betrayal of God is forgiven on the cross of Christ (Eph. 1:7).

Our being beloved to God, and the grace of God that found us and restored us out of conflict is the same grace that can move us out of conflict with one another, help us find one another, and restore us to each other when there is conflict in our relationships and in our community.

Grace is needed in our conflicts. Specifically, showing grace out of God's grace toward us as His beloved.

GRACE AMONG THE BELOVED'S CONFLICTS

We should not be surprised that difficulties and even conflict happen in the church. Conflicts inevitably and regularly pop up in any community that has been together for a significant period of time. The important thing to say here is that, as the beloved, we must not be resigned to stay in this space. Doing so will inevitably warp us and swallow us up, leaving nothing in the relationship but the conflict.

A church community involves being in spiritual relationships that require us to be intimate and open with others so that we can be one with them. As such, when there are problems and when there is sin, the state of affairs can easily solidify and become like a cement block hanging around the neck of the relationships in the community. Over time, more and more blocks get added around the neck, leaving relationships frozen and locked in place. Such a situation generates hostility, disconnection, and ultimately rejection as is found in a marriage that is defined by conflict.

No wonder that in situations like this, relationships break apart, churches split, and people end up leaving behind those they may have known for years or even decades.

What's needed in situations like this is a means to move past whatever barriers or hurts exist and to have a way to heal and repair relationships. What's needed is grace. Human beings on their own, however, do not naturally "evolve" toward grace. Conflict exists and persists because of our tendency to not show grace, to not

> **The grace of God is essential to any discussion about grace within the church.**

extend outsized goodness and kindness, to not offer opportunities for forgiveness and reconciliation. It's easier and feels safer to maintain the no-man's-land between the opposing party than to risk crossing it.

This is why the grace of God is so essential to any discussion about grace within the church. The grace of God that brings us into relationship with God also sustains us and maintains our life together before God.

Paul says, for example, "By the grace of God I am what I am" (1 Cor. 15:10). Luke in Acts 14:26 says Antioch is where Paul and Barnabas "had been commended to the grace of God for the work which they had fulfilled" (Acts 14:26), i.e., the mission work of Paul and Barnabas depended on God's continuing grace. When Paul talks in 2 Corinthians 12 about a persistent problem he had and the weakness it put into his life, he says he is able to handle it because of the sufficiency of God's grace for him, which is shown in how God's power is made perfect in weakness. In 1 Peter 4:10, we are told to use our gifts to serve one another "as good stewards of God's varied grace."

> **Grace in the church means we keep the channels of communication open. We jump on the chance to be favorable and do good to each other.**

Everything about who we are in relation to God and as the people of God comes from drawing out of the deep reservoir of God's grace.

So naturally, to talk about showing grace toward one another, we are talking about showing the grace of God to one another. That in the same way God has related to us, we relate to one another by generously being kind to one another and doing good for one another.

Grace, and specifically the grace of God in us, means that we don't easily abandon relationships. It means we create space and opportunity to be amenable to the other person. It means we always have channels by which we might rebuild that which is true and good and beautiful between us.

Grace in the church means we keep the channels of communication open. We jump on the chance to be favorable and do good to each other, knowing that such chances steadily chip away at whatever concrete blocks of conflict are dragging down our relationships.

Grace is how a beloved love remains among us. Grace is why God set His love upon us and it stays there because it bonds itself to our relationship with Him. If we try and move away from God, His love follows us and finds us, no matter where we might twist or turn away from God. God sees us and goes after us, even as we try to lose Him in the dark forest of our conflict. God's love always picks up the trail and keeps after us until He finds us and restores us back to Himself. When Romans 8:39 tells us that nothing can separate us from the love of God in Christ Jesus, this includes even our best attempts to fight against God, disconnect from, or reject Him.

TOOLS OF GRACE

A gracious love like this enables us to always be able to reset our relationships and restore them to health and wholeness. It gives us the creative tools to do whatever is needed.

One such tool is sacrifice. Picture two towns that once had an open road between them for easy access. The gates were wide open. But now the road is full of land mines. The gates are closed, and a massive wall has been built up around each town. The longer this situation goes on, the more reason there is for each town's population to stay safe and secure behind their own barriers. That is what it's like when conflict and then separation comes between two people or groups. The only way to break the stalemate is for someone to take the risk, to give up their comfort and security and leave their fortified town, walk over to the other town, and knock on the gate.

This of course is what God has done. The sacrifice of the Son is at the heart of the gospel. It is God in the person of Jesus putting Himself at risk to come to our side, even sacrificing His life to make it through to us. The sacrifice of the Son is the definitive act of God's grace, all so that we might be in relationship with Him.

Ephesians 5:25–26 directly states this sacrifice was the sacrifice of a husband on behalf of his bride, a gracious act of love in order that she, the church, might be presented before Him as the perfect holy partner to unite to her Lord. Every time we take Communion, we are reminded that the Lord, our husband, loved us so much He was willing to give up His body, indeed His entire life, to save us, His bride. The great nineteenth-century preacher Charles Spurgeon put it like this: "He loved you with such a love that he could not stop in heaven without you; he would sooner die than that you should perish; he stripped himself to nakedness that he might clothe you with beauty; he bowed his face to shame and spitting that he might lift you up to honour and glory."[2]

The way the Lord was willing to graciously give up all of Himself for His bride is the way we on that same basis are enabled to graciously give whatever is needed for the sake of healing and restoring relationship.

Sacrificial grace can be displayed in many ways. It could be willingness to sacrifice time to spend in conversation with someone. It could require the sacrifice of resources in order to rectify a wrong committed.

Fundamentally, however, sacrificial grace comes down to a willingness to let go of one's pride and adopt a posture of humility and openness to others within the community. As in the illustration above of the towns behind walls, someone needs to take the risk in order to bridge the impasse. Pride within us is like an ever-expanding balloon inside a locked car. It continues to grow and grow until nothing and no one can get in. We need to "pop" the balloon of pride in order for us to have space to allow someone in to connect with us. Popping our pride is a violent act, a sacrifice. But one worth making once we see how it is only in receiving others into our lives—daring intimacy and intentional presence—that we become the kind of community, and bride, we were created to be.

Another tool of gracious love is forgiveness. At our church, one of our values is being "grace motivated," and we describe it like this: "We show kindness and favor to one another while being willing to forgive and eager to bless each other."

Eager to bless each other means we are predisposed to look out for one another, to say good things and do good things in ways that will benefit one another.

Willing to forgive means when conflict happens we look for ways to reconcile, to address what's gone wrong and do whatever we can so that there can be forgiveness and ongoing relationship.

This is the hardest part of loving others through conflict. Which is again why the basis of this is God's gracious forgiveness of us, born out of His deep abiding beloved love for us. As Geoffrey Bromiley explains, "It is a forgiving and self-giving love that refuses to be defeated by the resistance of the beloved but steadfastly persists and conquers."[3]

It is because God forgives in this way that we then are able to extend the same forgiving love to one another.

This forgiving love, though, is not a doormat kind of forgiveness, whereby someone can walk back into the relationship without doing anything. Grace that extends forgiveness must be met by confession and repentance. God pursues us, but repentance is when we no longer run as hard away from Him, but instead finally stop and admit that we have been running away from Him. God's love and grace takes over from there, once we can admit what we've been doing. But we have to stop running, and we have to admit what we've been doing.

Grace to forgive must be matched by confession and repentance. If we extend grace to forgive someone, that someone in turn can only receive it upon their confession of the wrong and a commitment to repent, to live differently so that the wrong is not committed again.

GRACE IN COMPLEX, EMBEDDED CONFLICT

I periodically am asked about leading a diverse church—what it involves, how to do it. And the answer to those questions is that it is pretty hard. It's certainly much harder than I expected when we started in 2005. And arguably, leading and maintaining a diverse church seems like it should be pretty much impossible to do today. We simply have too many differences and divisions in our country. It is significantly easier to cater entirely to one particular ethnic, social, and class demographic. And, in all honesty, there can be legitimate, enjoyable community if you do focus on just one demographic of people.

At the same time, we should say it is still possible, and still needed, for there to be diverse communities of faith that cross ethnic, social, and class boundaries. Certainly, the first-century church bought into that vision. And we all know that this is the ultimate community we will be part of in the new heaven and new earth. Miroslav Volf writes,

> A catholic [i.e., a microcosm of the new creation] personality is a personality enriched by otherness, a personality which is what it is only because multiple others have been reflected in it in a particular way. The distance from my own culture that results from being born by the Spirit creates a fissure in me through which others can come in. The Spirit unlatches the doors of my heart saying: "You are not only you; others belong to you too."[4]

So what might we do now to establish and maintain a diverse church despite some difficulties or conflicts that seem inherent? The one absolutely essential ingredient, the one that gives us any hope for doing this kind of thing, is grace. A church whose people engage one another with grace is a church that has within it the means to navigate its relationships, especially where there is difference and conflict. Grace orients us automatically to show favor to one another. Grace provides the blueprint for when we have conflict with one another.

In church conflict, there are options available to us. We can fight back, determined to win. We can choose to gossip to other people about the person we are in conflict with. We can nurse a simmering

Because we relate to one another in the context of God's story of pursuing us, His bride in Jesus, then we can always look at our relational conflicts with a confident hope. For God's efforts and God's story always end in redemption and restoration.

grudge over an issue for countless months or years. All are potential options, but they don't eliminate the conflict; they just provide ways to navigate it.

Grace is the one and only option that can actually eliminate conflict. It is the only option that can heal, restore, and strengthen relationships through even the worst conflicts. For as we continue to show grace to one another even after there has been reconciliation, we build up the bank of love for one another that we can draw from the next time there is conflict. As Peter says, "Above all, *keep loving* one another earnestly, since love covers a multitude of sins" (1 Peter 4:8). Consistent love shown in continued grace toward one another helps us before, during, and after conflict.

If our relationship with one another were only tied to our personal efforts and experiences, we would always at some level feel uncertain about our relationships when they face conflict. We can't be sure if there can be healing, and we will have doubt or return to the same types of conflict even when we think things have been resolved.

But because our relationships are tied to God's efforts to be in relationship with us—because we relate to one another in the context of God's story of pursuing us, His bride in Jesus—then we can always look at our relational conflicts with a confident hope. For God's efforts and God's story always end in redemption and restoration, which means our efforts and our story in Him and through Him will also end the same way: continuing to be beloved to one another.

Dr. Martin Luther King Jr. offers helpful insight on the love of God being used to deal with conflict. He writes,

> Love is creative and redemptive. Love builds up and unites; hate tears down and destroys. The aftermath of the "fight with fire" method . . . is bitterness and chaos,

the aftermath of the love method is reconciliation and creation of the beloved community. Physical force can repress, restrain, coerce, destroy, but it cannot create and organize anything permanent; only love can do that. Yes, love—which means understanding, creative, redemptive goodwill, even for one's enemies—is the solution to the race problem.[5]

If there is one issue that has been a severe test for relationships within the American church, it is the "race problem." Race relations have been and continue to be one of the biggest conflicts between people in this country and within the church. It's a complex issue that requires an honest look at our own hearts and telling the truth about our racist past and its continued influence on the present.

However, over all this, for the Christian there should be a sense that even here, indeed especially here, we always have the means to deal with the conflicts that arise over race. If the Lord can look at us—the spouse who was hostile, disconnected, rejecting of Him, the spouse who over and over again betrayed Him—and yet still desire us and resolve conflict between us and Him and still make us His beloved, then we, having been loved like this, can love one another in the same way. That there can be beloved relationship in the most intractable conflicts, and yes, even between the oppressed and the racist oppressor.

> **Those who travel this road will enter into a new category of relating to one another in the beloved love of God, a way that can actually work and can really last.**

Being beloved to the Lord means God has made a way for the oppressed and the oppressor to leave behind their relational conflict and step into the loving embrace of God and, having experienced and known this embrace, step into the embrace of one another. They do this not by ignoring what brought conflict between them. They must directly address what has happened and do the work of repentance and repair in order to restore the relationship.

Dr. King's commitment to nonviolence was a tangible expression of the grace of God. Dr. King's intent was to set the table for restoration once the oppressor was willing to sit down with humility and willing to fully repent and do the work of repair rather than engage in continued hostility. Once that happened, both could walk away from the table no longer as oppressor and oppressed but as beloved to one another in the Lord.

As King writes, "Nonviolent resistance does not seek to defeat or humiliate the opponent, but to win his friendship and understanding. The nonviolent resister must often express his protest through noncooperation or boycotts, but he realizes that noncooperation and boycotts are not ends themselves; . . . The end is redemption and reconciliation."[6] He also wrote, "The aftermath of nonviolence is the creation of the beloved community, so that when the battle is over, a new relationship comes into being between the oppressed and the oppressor."[7]

As we mentioned, to move into the beloved embrace of the Lord requires grace, with sacrifice and confession and repentance. The same will be required for us to have loving embrace with one another. Those who travel this road will enter into a new category of relating to one another in the beloved love of God, a way that can actually work and can really last. May we strive toward this end.

Chapter 11

PERSEVERANCE

I ran track in high school and college. I ran as a sprinter, which means I ran short distances: 100, 200, 400 meters.

I enjoyed running, as long as it meant being able to sprint—going full speed and trying to keep at full speed over a short distance. I hated running when it wasn't sprinting. However, to be a good sprinter at short distances, I had to regularly train at longer distances. For example, one common practice we had in my college team was to go out and run at medium speed for four to five miles. I hated those practices. My body was built for distances measured in 100 to 400 meters. It was not built for running several miles.

Running several miles requires a different mindset than sprinting. When you sprint, you are focused on moving your body in sync as quickly as possible. This is especially true at the shortest distance I ran, 100 meters. There isn't much time to think beyond getting across those 100 meters as fast as possible. But when you are running miles instead of meters, there is a whole lot more time to be aware of what you are doing and to feel the pain of what you are doing. If you're running outdoors, you might have to navigate difficult terrain or weather changes. It will take more time; you can't reach the end of four miles in only ten seconds like in a 100-meter sprint. In a word, running several miles requires perseverance. It's the willingness to keep going, to keep your momentum going forward, to not give up but keep running.

Of course, it's not perseverance if we are talking about doing something enjoyable. I don't call it perseverance when I am doing our family's annual Star Wars movie marathon. That's pure enjoyment. What makes perseverance distinctly perseverance is that you persist, you continue on and keep going, in spite of significant challenges that threaten or tempt you to slow down or quit. We persevere when we endure and continue on in spite of the trial, the challenge, the difficulty of the current moment.

"NEVER STOPPING, NEVER GIVING UP"

Many of the best experiences in life require perseverance. If you want to ride the best rides at Disneyland, you will need to persevere as you wait in a long line. If you want to get to the bottom of the Grand Canyon, you will need to persevere as you descend through a long and difficult hike. If you want to graduate from high school and then from college or trade school, you will need to persevere through a slew of classes and assignments and tests.

And if you want to experience the benefits of a long-lasting relationship like marriage, you need to persevere. No marriage travels across a straight and flat path. Every marriage will encounter a myriad of obstacles and challenges. Some come from outside pressures or unexpected life events: the loss of a job, infertility struggles, sudden illness. Others come from internal difficulties: lack of time together, misunderstandings from unsaid expectations, poor communication. These obstacles have the potential to ensnare and derail a marriage. If a marriage is to continue, the husband and wife have to decide to stick with each other, to still show up in the marriage even when it's difficult, even when it's uncomfortable. They must have the will to persevere, to endure and continue on, patiently moving forward until they have come through on the other side of whatever obstacle or challenge they are facing in that moment.

Once again, we look to the marriage between God and His people to find our best example of perseverance. Not surprisingly, this marriage has required perseverance, and it has come specifically from God. As we've noted, the relationship between God and His people was rocky early on. It regularly faced difficult challenges and obstacles as the people of God doubted Him or outright defied Him or simply forgot about Him.

The main reason the relationship lasts is because of God's perseverance. In an earlier chapter we spoke about the Lord's commitment to us. To add to that, we can say that this commitment to us is born out of His perseverance. The Lord sticks with us, continues to live with us, to be married to us, no matter what.

Many times we see God described as one who loves with faithfulness and persistence.

I have loved you with an everlasting love; therefore I have continued my faithfulness to you. (Jer. 31:3)

The steadfast love of the LORD never ceases; his mercies never come to an end. (Lam. 3:22)

Give thanks to the LORD, for he is good, for his steadfast love endures forever. (Ps. 136:1)

The Jesus Storybook Bible is popular for children in many homes. Early on, author Sally Lloyd-Jones introduces a phrase that becomes a tagline throughout the rest of this children's Bible.

She writes about how God loves us with a "Never Stopping, Never Giving Up, Unbreaking, Always and Forever Love."[1]

It's a memorable phrase. It says that God's love is a persevering love. His love actively seeks us out, and once His love finds us it stays with us and never lets go of us, no matter what happens. This love is an always and forever love because it is love that comes out of God's commitment to persevere with us.

This is not to suggest that God is "blinded" by His love for us. That God is a kind of lovesick doormat that is putting up with being in a toxic relationship with us. God being with us is not an affirmation for the relationship to remain in the status quo. God perseveres with us with the intention of our growing and changing. In that sense, God's presevering love is a love that is sticking with us through whatever it takes until we get to a better place in our relationship with Him. His love is a patient, enduring love that intends to lead toward that end where we will be His holy and pure bride. With that end in sight, Rebecca McLaughlin writes that God's love sticks with us as it "sees our faults and lies and petty moral ugliness" and that it "sees us to the core and loves us still."[2]

"ALWAYS AND FOREVER LOVE"

So when we ask then how we might persevere in the relationships we have within our churches, the answer is obvious. We persevere in and through God's persevering love. Once again, we lean not on our ability to persevere in our relationships, but the Lord's ability to persevere in His relationship with us, letting that be the basis and means by which we can persevere with one another. God's "never stopping, never giving up, unbreaking, always and forever love" cements us to Him, and in so doing, cements us to one another.

Over time there can be many reasons to leave a relationship rather than endure (and sometimes these reasons are legitimate, as we humans living in a fallen world understand). This feels especially true right now to relationships within the church. Our relationships within the church today sometimes seem as durable as a soap bubble, which is flimsy to begin with and will pop with the slightest poke.

The various trials and tensions of the past few years have well proven this. A global pandemic. Racial unrest and protest marches over racial injustice. An increasingly secular culture. Divisive election cycles. Any one of these things is a strain to relationships within the church. Having them all happen in the last few years has done more than strain relationships—it has entirely severed many of them.

This is why the Lord and His persevering love is especially helpful to apply within our relationships as the beloved. Our relationship with the Lord has been full of betrayal, breaking of commitments, attaching ourselves to other partners but the Lord. As such, we have found ourselves drifting away from the Lord, letting other things crowd our affections and grab the attention of our hearts.

Love within any church community will be tested over and over again; by conflict; by passiveness; by apathy; by outside pressures and cultural tensions.

Love within any church community will be tested over and over again. It will be tested by conflict among church members. It will be tested by passiveness from church leaders. It will be tested by apathy born from the times we feel disconnected from our church. It will be tested by outside pressures and cultural tensions.

Our relationships with one another can persist through such testing when we realize that the love that is within our church is God's beloved love for us, and it is a persevering, never giving up, always and forever love. As we read in Romans 8, nothing in all creation is able to separate us from the love of God in Christ Jesus our Lord. *Nothing.* Not even the worst problems and tensions and conflicts and difficulties. Not even the longest stretches of listless church meetings and awkward worship services. Not even the failures to act proactively or respond fully to needs among us. Not even church splits or church scandals. Not even hypocritical leaders or legalistic church members.

> **God's persevering love creates the time and space for us to always find Him again; so also we—when we love with this same love—create the same time and space for us to find one another again and again.**

Just as none of those things can keep us from God's love, so none of them should keep us from our relationships as the beloved with one another. Our relationships are based on the same persevering, enduring love described in Romans 8.

This is not to suggest that problems or difficulties or obstacles or failures are being ignored for the sake of "perseverance." What we are talking about is a love that is willing to endure with another person even as at the same time we press for the necessary conversations and actions that will help bring forgiveness and reconciliation or understanding and empathy that might heal, repair, restore, and ultimately refresh our relationships for the long haul till we reach eternity. God's persevering love creates the time and space for us to always find Him again; so also we—when we love with this same love—create the same time and space for us to find one another again and again.

HIKING WITH HOPE

Havasu Falls in Arizona is one of the most beautiful waterfalls you will ever see. People come from all over to see it and experience it by swimming around in the crystal clear, turquoise blue water that the falls pour into.

It's a beautiful place, but you can't directly reach it. There is no way to drive there or stroll over for a look. You can only get to it by hiking for ten miles. This is a serious hike, one that will take you at least four hours, usually more. Throughout the hike you might wonder if you are going in the right direction, as there is nothing to suggest that you are about to come upon a waterfall. The difficulty and length of the hike can even tempt you to give up.

People who set out on this journey do so not because of what they see immediately in front of them but because of the pictures they have seen and what others have told them of what they will eventually see and experience . . . as long as they persist in hiking on the predetermined path. They go on this hike with the certain hope that if they can endure and devote the time needed, they will be rewarded with the experience of these spectacular falls.

So how do we endure and persist long enough that space can be created to heal and restore our relationships? It happens the more sure and clear you are about where the relationship is headed.

As difficult and challenging and unsure relationships within the church can be, it's important that we keep in front of us this clear picture of where ultimately all such relationships are headed—united in joyful worship of God and enjoyment of Him and one another forever in His presence.

Jesus died and then rose from the dead in order to ensure this will happen. Nothing can stop it from happening. In His death and resurrection, we already are betrothed to Him. The marriage supper we will have together with the Lord is already planned and the table set. "Let us rejoice and exult and give him the glory, for the marriage of the Lamb has come, and his Bride has made herself ready" (Rev. 19:7).

This is the hope we need to persevere in our relationships. We endure through these relationships because this is the final destination for us, His beloved, and the beloved of one another. And because God is the one who has secured it, He ensures that we will eventually get there.

CLOSING THOUGHTS

This book was born out of asking the question, So how has God loved us? More specifically, what is one of the strongest and broadest and deepest ways to describe how God has loved us?

The answer to that is to say God loves us like a husband loves his wife. God has come to us in Jesus in order to make us His bride. This kind of love speaks to enduring commitment, to intimate union, to delightful affection. No one else in the universe can say that they are loved like this. Only human beings can say they are loved in this way and to this degree.

And because we belong to God, because we are the body of Christ, we love based on this love. In the same way we belong to God in His love, we belong to one another in His love. In the same way we were made into the body of Christ by His love, we will remain the body of Christ by His love.

Because we belong to God and are the body of Christ, there is no separation between our love for one another and God's love for us. Our love is a part of God's love. God's love is where everything starts, and out of that flows all other loves, like our love for one another in the church. Roberta Bondi says it well:

For [early Christian monastics], God's love, their love
of God, the love of God extended to them through
their communities, and their love with which they desired to love others, all these were the same love. God's
love was primary; out of God's love for them flowed all
other love.[1]

And once God's love is flowing among us, not only does it
connect us together, it also moves us together toward communion with God and with one another forever. We might imagine,
then, God's love as a river that eventually pours into a lake that
stretches out beyond what any of us can see. This lake is forever
life with God and with one another where "we will be united to
Him and to each other in an ecstasy of love and delight compared with which the most rapturous love between a man and a
woman on this earth is mere milk and water."[2]

Because it is eternity with the infinite God, there is no end to
what we will know, learn, and experience from God and from one
another. We will know God and one another, expressing affection
for Him and for one another in rapturous ways, in wonderfully
deep and delightful and intimate ways on a Monday in heaven.
And then Tuesday will come and we will find that what we experienced on Monday already falls far short of what we will then
come to know and feel and experience on that Tuesday. Tuesday
will bring an even more invigorating, more transformative experience of divine love among us and God. Tuesday will come to a
close, Wednesday will start, and within the first few moments we
already will have surpassed what we experienced the previous
two days. And so it will go, day after day, month after month,
year after year. It's a kind of married life with God and with one
another where no sin or sickness or death can disrupt or degrade
the life we have together.

This is the future for us. Our present is a signpost toward that future. It is also an early chapter of that future. Our salvation in Christ isn't only a promise that we live within divine love. It is the entrance into divine love. Our efforts to love one another out of this same love are already part of eternity.

This means that any effort to love out of this strong and deep expression of God's love will eventually work. His beloved love is already a guarantee of success when deployed in any relationship and any community. Any tensions or problems or divisions we have within the church, seen in this light, become "light and momentary" afflictions, destined to fall in the face of our Lord's massive love.

With Paul then, let's pray that a beloved love "may abound more and more" and that we'll "increase and abound in love for one another" (Phil: 1:9; 1 Thess. 3:12), hastening the day when all that remains are people feasting and rejoicing together in the love of our Beloved Lord.

ACKNOWLEDGMENTS

There are many to thank for helping and supporting me in the writing and publishing of this book. I could mention almost everyone I've had a relationship with over my entire life. So here are some thanks to a few among the many I could thank.

Thank you Trillia Newbell for giving me the opportunity to write this book.

Thank you Pam Pugh for your editing. This book is a lot better because of your work on it.

Thank you to the Moody team in general, for your support and investment in me to get this book out.

Thank you Roosevelt Community Church, for supporting me in the writing of this book and being a church that continues to be dedicated to being a beloved community.

Thanks in particular to my fellow pastors, Bob Korljan and John Talley III, for giving me the time and space to write on this topic and teach and preach on it.

Thank you to James Nwobu for helping me come up with the book title.

Thank you John Onwuchekwa for answering my many text messages to help me figure out the book subtitle and cover image.

Thank you to my extended family, in particular my mom Adeline for the faith she passed on to me and my sister Melissa.

Thank you to my kids, Marcel, Mya, Judah, Jovanna, Rosa—for being my crazy kids! May you experience the Lord's love in even stronger and sweeter ways than I have.

Thank you to my wife Dennae—for loving me so strongly and fully.

NOTES

INTRODUCTION

1. Ezra Klein, *Why We're Polarized* (New York, NY: Avid Reader Press, 2020).

2. The Greek speaking Jews versus the Hebraic Jews in Acts 6, the poor Christians versus the wealthy Christians alluded to in James and Romans 14, and the Gentile Christians versus the Jewish Christians in 1 Corinthians 15 are a few examples from the early church.

CHAPTER 1: BELOVED TO THE LORD

1. Jonathan Edwards, "The Church's Marriage to Her Sons, and to Her God," in *Works of Jonathan Edwards*, 25:187. Quoted in Jonathan King, *The Beauty of the Lord: Theology as Aesthetics* (Bellingham, WA: Lexham Press, 2018), 292.

2. "It was more than a mere legal contract. It is a covenant between man and wife before God which is a harbinger of the covenant between God and his people. This covenantal character of marriage entails that it is a sacred bond that is characterized by permanence, sacredness, intimacy, mutuality and exclusiveness. From what is said we see that the husband 'gave [a] solemn oath' (pledged faith) to the wife and entered into a covenant not intended to be broken. Significantly, the biblical marriage ceremony was a joyous public event in which the two partners solemnized their covenant with God and community." Alby Thomas, "Marriage and Family in the Bible," August 25, 2016, www.academia.edu/27994858/Marriage/_and/_Family/_in/_the/_Bible?email_work_card=title.

3. Seock-Tae Sohn, *YHWH, the Husband of Israel: The Metaphor of Marriage between YHWH and Israel* (Eugene, OR: Wipf and Stock, 2002), 49.

4. Ibid., 85.

5. Ibid., 82. Also see Daniel I. Block, *Covenant: The Framework of God's Grand Plan of Redemption* (Grand Rapids, MI: Baker Academic, 2021), 143, 374.

6. God talks about giving "a decree of divorce" to the northern kingdom as a warning to the southern kingdom of Israel in Jeremiah 3:8–10.

7. Aimee Byrd, "Freedom to Ask for What We Want: Part 2," October 29, 2021, www.aimeebyrd.com/2021/10/28/freedom-to-ask-for-what-we-want-part-2.

8. Eric Ortlund, "The Wisdom of the Song of Songs: A Pastoral Guide for Preaching and Teaching," *Themelios* 45, no. 3, https://www.thegospelcoalition.org/themelios/article/the-wisdom-of-the-song-of-songs-a-pastoral-guide-for-preaching-and-teaching/.

9. Ibid.

10. "The Song hints at a greater Love standing behind human romance and the total commitment with which he relates to us, a Love stronger than death, jealous beyond the grave, unquenchable, fierce, not to be denied." Ortlund, "The Wisdom of the Song of Songs."

11. Raymond C. Ortlund Jr., *God's Unfaithful Wife: A Biblical Theology of Spiritual Adultery* (Downers Grove, IL: 1996), 173.

CHAPTER 2: BELOVED TO ONE ANOTHER

1. Martin Luther King Jr., *Strength to Love* (Minneapolis, MN: Fortress Press, 2010), 152.

2. M. Robert Mulholland Jr., *The Deeper Journey: The Spirituality of Discovering Your True Self* (Downers Grove, IL: InterVarsity Press, 2006), 128.

3. Christopher Morgan, ed., *The Love of God* (Wheaton, IL: Crossway, 2016), 88.

4. Ibid., 131.

5. "Christian action is therefore a being taken up into God's action through grace, being taken up into God's love so that one can love with him." Hans Urs von Balthasar, *Love Alone Is Credible* (San Francisco, CA: St. Ignatius Press, 2016), 116.

CHAPTER 3: INITIATIVE

1. Seock-Tae Sohn, *YHWH, the Husband of Israel: The Metaphor of Marriage between YHWH and Israel* (Eugene, OR: Wipf and Stock, 2002), 14.
2. Ibid., 82.
3. Matthew Haste, "Your Maker Is Your Husband: The Divine Marriage Metaphor and the New Covenant," *Puritan Reformed Journal* 5, no. 1 (2013): 18.
4. Raymond C. Ortlund Jr., *God's Unfaithful Wife: A Biblical Theology of Spiritual Adultery* (Downers Grove, IL: 1996), 67.

CHAPTER 4: WORDS

1. Lauren Winner, *Real Sex: The Naked Truth about Chastity* (Grand Rapids, MI: Brazos Press, 2006), 146.

CHAPTER 6: INTIMACY

1. Seock-Tae Sohn, *YHWH, the Husband of Israel: The Metaphor of Marriage between YHWH and Israel* (Eugene, OR: Wipf and Stock, 2002), 19.
2. Timothy J. Keller, The Timothy Keller Sermon Archive, Redeemer Presbyterian Church, 2013.
3. Richard Beck, *Unclean: Meditations on Purity, Hospitality, and Mortality* (Eugene, OR: Cascade, 2011), 114.
4. John DelHousaye, *The Fourfold Gospel, Volume 2: A Formational Commentary on Matthew, Mark, Luke, and John* (Eugene, OR: Pickwick Publications, 2021), 350.
5. Hans Urs von Balthasar, *Prayer* (San Francisco, CA: St. Ignatius Press, 1986), 38–41.

CHAPTER 7: PRESENCE

1. J. Scott Duvall and J. Daniel Hays, *God's Relational Presence: The Cohesive Center of Biblical Theology* (Grand Rapids, MI: Baker Academic, 2019), 16.
2. "YHWH's dwelling among the Israelites can be compared to that of a newly wedded couple in their home. YHWH's dwelling in the midst of Israel reinforces the analogy of a marriage relationship between them. The visible symbol of his residence among the Israelites was his tabernacle placed in the midst of Israel's tents and the people of Israel understood the presence of YHWH through the tabernacle's existence among them." Seock-Tae Sohn, *YHWH, the Husband of Israel: The Metaphor of Marriage between YHWH and Israel* (Eugene, OR: Wipf and Stock, 2002), 34.
3. Ibid., 52.
4. The Berean Bible, public domain.
5. Scot McKnight, *A Fellowship of Differents: Showing the World God's Design for Life Together* (Grand Rapids, MI: Zondervan, 2015), 56.
6. Christine Pohl, *Making Room: Recovering Hospitality as a Christian Tradition* (Grand Rapids, MI: Eerdmans, 1999), quoting Jualynne E. Dodson and Cheryl Townsend Gilkes in "There's Nothing Like Church Food," *Journal of the American Academy of Religion* 63, no. 3 (Fall 1995): 519–38.

CHAPTER 8: COMMITMENT

1. Seock-Tae Sohn, *YHWH, the Husband of Israel: The Metaphor of Marriage between YHWH and Israel* (Eugene, OR: Wipf and Stock, 2002), 31.
2. Ibid., 64.
3. Joseph H. Hellerman, *When the Church Was a Family: Recapturing Jesus' Vision for Authentic Christian Community* (Nashville, TN: B&H Publishing Group, 2009), 35–36, 39–40.
4. In the Pentateuch specifically and throughout the rest of the Old Testament, marriage is called a covenant (*berith*). (See Ex. 20:5;

34:14; Lev. 26:12; Deut. 5:9; 29:13; Josh. 24:19; Prov. 2:14, 17; Ezek. 16:8, 59–62; Hos. 2:2; Mal. 2:14). David Instone-Brewer, *Divorce and Remarriage in the Bible: The Social and Literary Context* (Grand Rapids, MI: Eerdmans, 2002).

5. Alby Thomas, "Marriage and Family in the Bible," August 25, 2016, www.academia.edu/27994858/Marriage/_and/_Family/_in/_the/_Bible?email_work_card=title.

6. David Strain, "Is Attending a Wedding an Endorsement?," The Gospel Coalition, March 3, 2022, www.thegospelcoalition.org/article/attending-wedding-endorsement.

7. Rebecca McLaughlin, *Confronting Jesus: 9 Encounters with the Hero of the Gospels* (Wheaton, IL: Crossway, 2022), 115.

8. Matthew Haste, "Your Maker Is Your Husband: The Divine Marriage Metaphor and the New Covenant," *Puritan Reformed Journal* 5, no. 1 (2013): 19.

9. Derek Kidner, *The Message of Hosea* (Downers Grove, IL: IVP Academic, 1984), 34. Cited by Matthew Haste, "Your Maker Is Your Husband."

10. Raymond C. Ortlund Jr., *God's Unfaithful Wife: A Biblical Theology of Spiritual Adultery* (Downers Grove, IL: 1996), 70–71.

11. J. S. Kselman, s.v. "Grace: Old Testament," in David Noel Freedman, ed., *The Anchor Yale Bible Dictionary*, D–G: Volume 2 (New York, NY: Doubleday, 1992), 1086.

12. First published in 2000 and updated in 2020, Robert Putnam's observations are still in play, perhaps even more so with the proliferation of social media.

13. In fact, many of the past creeds have us say things that speak directly to our mutual commitment to the Lord. Note for instance how the first response in a creed like the Heidelberg Catechism reminds believers that they belong not to themselves but to Christ. To recite this as a community reinforces the community's mutual commitment to one another in their mutual commitment to Christ.

CHAPTER 9: PASSION

1. Daniel I. Block, *Covenant: The Framework of God's Grand Plan of Redemption* (Grand Rapids, MI: Baker Academic, 2021), 137.
2. Walter Brueggemann, *An Unsettling God: The Heart of the Hebrew Bible* (Minneapolis, MN: Fortress Press, 2009), 22.
3. J. Alex Motyer in Thomas Edward McComiskey, ed., *Minor Prophets: A Commentary on Obadiah, Jonah, Micah, Nahum, Habakkuk* (Grand Rapids, MI: Baker Academic, 2018).
4. Raymond C. Ortlund Jr., "Is the God of the Old Testament a God of Love?," in *The Love of God*, ed. Christopher W. Morgan (Wheaton, IL: Crossway, 2016), 43.
5. "The intensity and depth of YHWH's relationship with his people was analogous to the marriage of a man and his wife, which accounts for the use of the expression *qin'a*, 'jealousy,' more properly translated as 'passion' in theological and covenantal contexts." Block, *Covenant*, 139.
6. Timothy J. Keller, The Timothy Keller Sermon Archive, Redeemer Presbyterian Church, 2013.
7. Ortlund, "Is the God of the Old Testament a God of Love?," 43.
8. David T. Lamb, *The Emotions of God: Making Sense of a God Who Hates, Weeps, and Loves* (Downers Grove, IL: InterVarsity Press, 2022), 157.
9. Eugene E. Carpenter and Philip Wesley Comfort, *Holman Treasury of Key Bible Words: 200 Greek and 200 Hebrew Words Defined and Explained* (Nashville, TN: Holman Reference, 2000), 96.
10. See 1 Thess. 2:17–20; 3:6, 10; 2 Tim. 1:4.

CHAPTER 10: CONFLICT

1. John Calvin, Institutes, 2.16. Cited by David Clyde Jones, *Biblical Christian Ethics* (Grand Rapids, MI: Baker, 1994), 48.
2. Charles H. Spurgeon, "A Jealous God," in *The Metropolitan Tabernacle Pulpit Sermons*, vol. 9, 191 (London: Passmore & Alabaster, 1863), 191.

3. Geoffrey W. Bromiley, *God and Marriage* (Grand Rapids, MI: Eerdmans, 1980), 31.
4. Miroslav Volf, *Exclusion & Embrace: A Theological Exploration of Identity, Otherness, and Reconciliation* (Nashville, TN: Abingdon Press, 2019), 43.
5. Martin Luther King Jr., *The Papers of Martin Luther King, Jr., Volume IV: Symbol of the Movement, January 1957–December 1958*, ed. Clayborne Carson (Oakland, CA: University of California Press, 2000).
6. Ibid., 139.
7. Clayborne Carson, ed., *The Autobiography of Martin Luther King, Jr.*, repr. ed. (New York, NY: Warner Books, 2001), 125.

CHAPTER 11: PERSEVERANCE

1. Sally Lloyd-Jones, *The Jesus Storybook Bible: Every Story Whispers His Name* (Grand Rapids, MI: Zonderkidz, 2007).
2. Rebecca McLaughlin, *Confronting Jesus: 9 Encounters with the Hero of the Gospels* (Wheaton, IL: Crossway, 2022), 119.

CLOSING THOUGHTS

1. Roberta Bondi, *To Love as God Loves: Conversations with the Early Church* (Philadelphia, PA: Fortress Press, 1987), 107.
2. C. S. Lewis, *Mere Christianity*, revised & enlarged edition (San Francisco, CA: Harper, 2001), 46.